BUSY AS F*CK

BUSY AS F*CK

KAREN NIMMO

HarperCollins_Publishers_

HarperCollins*Publishers*

First published in 2019
by HarperCollins*Publishers* (New Zealand) Limited
Unit D1, 63 Apollo Drive, Rosedale, Auckland 0632, New Zealand
harpercollins.co.nz

HarperCollins*Publishers*
Unit D1, 63 Apollo Drive, Rosedale, Auckland 0632, New Zealand
Level 13, 201 Elizabeth Street, Sydney NSW 2000, Australia
A 53, Sector 57, Noida, UP, India
1 London Bridge Street, London, SE1 9GF, United Kingdom
Bay Adelaide Centre, East Tower, 22 Adelaide Street West, 41st floor, Toronto,
  Ontario M5H 4E3, Canada
195 Broadway, New York NY 10007, USA

A catalogue record for this book is available from the National Library of New Zealand.

ISBN 978 1 7755 4144 8 (pbk)
ISBN 978 1 7754 9175 0 (ebook)

Cover design by Mark Campbell, HarperCollins Design Studio
Typeset in Sabon LT Std by Kirby Jones
Cover images by shutterstock.com
Printed and bound in Australia by McPherson's Printing Group
The papers used by HarperCollins in the manufacture of this book are a natural, recyclable
product made from wood grown in sustainable plantation forests. The fibre source and
manufacturing processes meet recognised international environmental standards, and carry
certification.

He aha te mea nui o te ao
What is the most important thing in the world?

He tangata, he tangata, he tangata
It is the people, it is the people, it is the people.
– Māori proverb

'The mind I love must have wild places, a tangled orchard where dark damsons drop in the heavy grass, an overgrown little wood, the chance of a snake or two, a pool that nobody's fathomed the depth of, and paths threaded with flowers planted by the mind.'
– Katherine Mansfield

A cautionary note
Busy as F*ck people walk among us. Actually, they *are* us.
While the stories, anecdotes and examples in this book are true,
all names and identifying details have been changed to protect
confidentiality. Where I suspected someone's story might be
recognisable I've blended details from several sources. If you
think you recognise yourself or someone else in these pages
please dismiss it as purely wishful thinking.

Contents

We're All As Busy As F*CK

Over lunch I met a Busy woman who gave me a detailed account of her busyness far beyond my level of interest.

As I listened my lifeblood ebbed away. So much to do, so little time: her work, her kids, her charities, her house, her parents, her everything. Her phone rang in her bag as she was talking. When she finally left me for someone more receptive I felt like screaming. Or drinking. Make that both.

But she was not an unpleasant woman, nor a mean one. She was just so trapped in her busyness she could not see outside it. Or understand that someone she had just met might not be so invested.

Busy, Busy, BUSY

Busy is our new normal. It sits slightly outside the Anxiety Club, even though it can affect our physical and emotional health in the same ways, because Busy people are not unwell; they've just got a to-do list that never ends.

They also look frighteningly like most of us.

Think about the last time someone asked you how you were? Did you hear yourself saying 'busy'?

1

I've certainly said it. It's partly habit, partly that we're almost scared not to say it. Because the opposite of busy is … well … no-one wants to be that. It implies no meaningful work, no friends, no activities, no life. What a loser.

I tried this with a group of friends. 'I'm not busy,' I said. It was true – I'd taken some time off work so my time was all, deliciously, my own.

There was a sort of uneasy silence then one friend rushed in to cover for me. 'But you're doing all sorts of other things.' Code for you're not lazy or a loser. You're busy too. Just In Your Own Way.

I took the leave pass graciously. I need my friends.

But really? When did busy become a badge of honour? I've never heard busy offered up at a funeral as a source of pride. 'We'll miss this Busy Woman. She led a life So Busy.' The saying is 'Rest in Peace' for a reason. My dream is that we are able to do it while we are alive.

But how? There's no dodging the reality of frenetic modern lifestyles and the related hit on our health and wellbeing. It worries me that we rush frantically between work and yoga classes; that we load our phones with meditation apps we don't have time to use; that we struggle to get our heart rates down to resting even when we *are* resting.

What's going on? When did it all get this crazy? How did we lose our way?

The developed world is awash with mental health difficulties; depression, anxiety and suicide are rising at alarming rates – and those are just the official numbers. As a clinical psychologist in private practice, I've witnessed the increase in referrals over the past decade as people knock up against the demands of their hectic lives: home, work, study, relationships and money. Traditionally, people sought help for classified mental disorders; now, in addition to those difficulties, therapy has become a melting pot of emotional struggle fused with the stuff of ordinary life. *Why am*

I constantly stressed? How do I stop feeling overwhelmed and exhausted? Why do I overthink everything? How can I be more motivated? More resilient? How can I COPE? How do I help my kids to do the same?

Everywhere you look people are rushed, exhausted, jittery, distracted, frustrated and unsatisfied. People in mid-life are weighed down by obligation and responsibility; young people, who should be excited by life, are paralysed by choice and loaded decisions. It used to be that we only had to keep up with the Joneses; now, with a 24/7 online window to the lives of others, we're in a competition we never signed on for, striving to do more, have more, be more. *Come on! Be productive. Don't waste a moment. Find your passion. Follow your star. Live the dream. Take better holidays. Make more money. Go to more parties. Date someone hotter. Post a cooler photo.* It's exhausting and unhealthy – not to mention a little weird.

We all know stress can be a good thing – motivating, even inspiring – and so a life without stress might mean we're selling ourselves short.

But we know, too, a stress overload can take us directly the other way.

When stress turns toxic, it swings a wrecking ball at our mental and physical health. Multiple studies have shown links between stress and sleep difficulties, heart disease, blood pressure problems, weakened immune systems, weight fluctuations and a raft of other physical health issues. Psychologically, depression and anxiety are the pack leaders, but stress can be implicated in the whole gambit of mental struggle.

But it can be hard to gauge the tipping point when we are all as Busy as F*ck, up to our necks with the demands of living. When we're running ragged from day-to-night-to-day-again without the space to reflect on what matters to us, to build lives that we feel proud of and invested in.

This book is a roadmap through all that stressing and striving. It's about trading in your Busy as F*ck lifestyle for something more meaningful. It's about facing life with a slower heart rate, a thicker skin and a sparkle in your eye – and being able to teach your kids the same things.

These are the steps you can take towards a calmer, more resilient life, based on clinical research and what has worked for my clients.

Think of it as do-it-yourself therapy – in 10 sessions – complete with tools and tactics to help you on your way. So are you ready? I can see your foot tapping and your fingers creeping towards your phone. It's time. Grab a seat on the couch and let's go.

Busy As F*ck Syndrome: What Is It and Do You Have It?

Extract from the *Diagnostic and Statistical Manual of Life (DSM-Life)*, 1st edition

Classification

Busy as F*ck Syndrome is a condition characterised by a cluster of symptoms, which overtax a person's emotional and physical capacity to the potential detriment of health, wellbeing and quality of life.

Differential Diagnosis (What Busy As F*ck Syndrome Is Not)

Busy as F*ck Syndrome is not a disease, mental deficiency or abnormality. You won't find it listed in any of the official diagnostic manuals because it does not exist as a bona fide mental disorder. It is simply a condition of our chaotic 21st century lifestyles.

Onset and prevalence; age and gender

Busy as F*ck Syndrome commonly presents in mid-life when professional, financial and family demands peak. It is notably trending up in adolescent and young adult populations as they navigate a complex and competitive world. While no official statistics exist (yet), it is estimated to occur in more than half the adult population, with a slightly higher incidence in women, in line with official anxiety statistics.

Environmental Pattern

Busy as F*ck Syndrome is prevalent in societies that heavily promote the worth of the individual over the group, perfectionism over 'good enough' and novelty over tradition. Vulnerability increases in domestic, work and social environments where productivity and mega-achievement are highly valued.

Psychosocial and Societal Factors (or How the World Has Changed)

Busy as F*ck Syndrome is influenced by a number of 21st century–specific factors. Here are the ones to watch for:

1. **There's so much to do.** We are working longer and reporting higher levels of work stress – all stress, as financial, family and work pressures collide. People are raising kids while their parents are still working, so families can't help each other like they used to. Then we're raising teenagers and caring for elderly parents at the same time. Technology and gadgets invented to make tasks easier have also given us more to do. How much time do you spend on technological problems?
2. **We're screenaholics.** Screens allow us to live, work and play *but* with the benefits come the pitfalls: online addiction is a big and growing concern. We rarely disconnect so we're always 'on', permanently distracted, jumping from task to task in a keyed-up state. Because we never fully come down or switch off, our brains and bodies don't get the quality rest they need to function at their best.

3. **We know what's happening in the world.** Global connectedness means we're hyper-aware of what's going on in the world: war, political and religious unrest, prejudice, racism, terrorism, natural disaster, poverty, sadness and fear. The cumulative effect of constant exposure weighs us down: while it's healthy to feel empathy for others, the world feels 'heavier' and more uncertain than a decade ago and it's filtering into our psyches.

4. **We've lost our physical communities.** We have access to online tribes (if we are lucky) and we can stay in touch with loved ones more easily, but we don't have the time to physically connect with groups or communities that gave us a sense of friendship, belonging and contribution. Most people simply don't have time or energy for community work or to volunteer at their clubs anymore.

5. **We know what everyone else is doing.** Social media means we can see what others are doing – whether we like it or not, whether we care about them or not. It has made us more prone to comparison, dissatisfaction and envy. It's a race without end, and there are no prizes.

6. **We want to be special (or we really don't want to be ordinary).** The developed world is individually driven, so we must strive for a Mighty Destiny: being ordinary and decent is not enough. We place ourselves at the centre of everything, and we orient everything back to ourselves. It keeps the focus on The Self, when it's healthier to look up and out.

Course and Outcomes (or the Good News)

Busy as F*ck Syndrome does not persist throughout life – unless we allow it to. It responds exceptionally well to consistent self-management. Sound emotional, resilience and relationship skills lead to positive, sustainable outcomes.

How to Self-Diagnose

Answer yes or no to the following statements:

- When people ask how you are your first word is BUSY.
- You don't stop at Busy. You begin to verbally process your thousands of obligations without noticing a pallor come over your subject's face. Even if you do, you press on.
- You consistently feel stressed, rushed and overwhelmed, so much so that you should be losing weight. But you're not. (You often eat while doing something else.)
- Your sleep patterns are erratic – either wakeful or coma-like – and most days you wake up feeling washed out and overwhelmed by the day ahead.
- You stay up too late. And every day you promise yourself you need to get to bed earlier – but you don't.
- You would rather teeter on the edge of insanity than fail at turning in that batch of muffins (or anything else) you promised. You are a person who *delivers*.
- You tell yourself you like being busy, that busy people get more done, even though when you look in the mirror you are frightened by the ghost staring back.
- You can't relax without social media or exercise (if you had time, but you mostly don't). Even a great book struggles to hold your attention.
- You are easily distracted, decisions stress you out, your memory doesn't seem what it was and you (secretly) worry about early onset dementia.
- You are excessively irritable, even over things that don't really matter. Even reading this is winding you up. Tap, tap, tap.

- Your to-do list keeps getting longer. You feel like you're in Survival Mode – constantly. Some days you don't think you can cope *but* you do. The next day ticks up, and off you go again ...

Results

If you answered yes to most of the questions, panic only slightly. Some life stages demand more of us than others. It's okay if you feel you are coping *and* this is how you want to live.

But these warning signs can morph into serious problems, so pay attention if your busyness is eroding your enjoyment of your people and activities, especially if it's negatively affecting your moods, emotional reactions and personality.

And – even if it's not – get your blood pressure checked. And read on – there are plenty of tips lying in wait for you!

The Biggest Sales Job of All

I was once called a crap dealer.

A young man I was working with was neck-deep in telling me about his cheating girlfriend, his manipulative mother and the job he was desperate to leave when he pulled up, mid-sentence: 'How do you even listen to all this? You're dealing in crap.'

His take on it still makes me smile. Clinical psychologists see life's struggles up close. While the dream is to help people create meaningful lives, the starting point is often pain. Very few people reach out, or look to make changes, when life is great. *Hey, I've just scored a fantastic new job, I've just met the person of my dreams, I've lost the weight I've been battling with for years – can you help me out with that?* Why would they? When things are going well we don't want to change them – despair, distress and worry are much bigger motivators. And in our Busy as F*ck worlds, those things are increasingly common.

Not everyone is distressed or unwell when they come through the door, but everyone has a problem to solve, an itch to scratch or an improvement to make. Always, they want something to be *better* or *different*. That's the bottom line of psychology: we go after change.

Most of my work has been with adults and adolescents, for individual therapy sessions, 55 minutes at a time. I've seen couples and family groups, too, not as a specialist, but in the normal flow of my practice. In sports and business I've worked as a performance coach, helping people iron out problems, get the best from themselves, go after their dreams. Frequently, therapy and coaching blend together.

While most people welcome the opportunity to gain insights and learn new skills, others apologise for stealing your time: *I shouldn't be here; so many people have tougher things to deal with than me.* That's a true statement – there will always be someone with a greater burden – but it's not a fair one. If someone sees it as a problem, then it's a problem. We don't have to rank our difficulties against what others are going through to make them valid. No lives are easy; every problem counts.

So that's the job, and I'm up for it.

But if I close my eyes I can still see a young TV salesman I worked with shortly after I qualified. Blond, pony-tailed and barely needing to shave, he was struggling with mood swings and anxiety, a spillover from a traumatic past. He had also just won the top sales award for his multinational company.

'How'd you get so good so fast?' I asked.

He looked at the floor, clamping a hand on the knee that had started to spasm. I suspected he wasn't used to praise. 'My old man. He was a useless father but he could sell *anything*. I reckon he'd have sold me if he could have got away with it.'

He paused, thinking. 'He used to say selling's not about products, it's about people. He'd bang on that everyone was in sales. I used to think he was full of it, but now I think he was right.'

'How's that? I'm not in sales.'

'Wait a minute,' he countered, looking at me steadily now. 'Yours is the biggest sales job of all. Come on, play the game – tell me what you're selling.'

I hesitated; we'd only just met and perhaps I didn't want to fail before I'd started. 'I guess I'm selling hope.'

He beamed at me like I'd just bought the biggest TV in his store.

It might be the best advice I ever got.

What's Up?

A young woman rushes into my office one morning. She skids to a halt and it crosses my mind that it's a good thing I have old carpet. These are not things I say out loud, at least not till I know someone and can lay reliable odds they will laugh.

Livvy is 30 years old, has a personal brand of corporate chic and is a marketing executive on the fast track. She describes a social life to rival the Kardashians, just as many social media connections, and a Fitbit that shows she's REM sleep-deprived and racks up 20,000-plus steps a day.

She perches on the edge of my couch like she's not staying long. She's a little breathless, she talks rapidly, her eyes dart around the room and one of her legs jiggles constantly up and down.

She's here for some help with anxiety and she's making ME nervous.

I don't tell her this, for I am supposed to be the epitome of chill, a person most qualified to walk the talk.

'How can I help you?' I say, as evenly as I can, turning limpet-like in my chair, in a bid to calm her down. Using your own physical presence to set the mood is a trick well known to body language gurus, but psychologists tend to apply it without thinking – just because it works.

'I can't sit still,' she says, with a wan smile.

No kidding, Livvy, I say with my eyes. I can feel my pulse beating in my temples.

'When I try to relax, I freak out I'm not getting enough done. I have to be productive, to *achieve* things. If I don't get lots done, it's a really bad day for me.'

I wait.

'But lately, it's all spun out of control. I can't find my off switch.'

Livvy has developed panic attacks and she has some rolling anxiety underneath it, but once we have alleviated those, I know we will be dealing with a scourge of modern life for which there has been no official term – until now.

Welcome to Busy as F*ck Syndrome.

Livvy sinks back into the couch: we have some work to do. But the 10 steps we are set to take are common to anyone who wants to make a change or improvement to their Busy as F*ck lifestyle – or who wants a tried and true roadmap to a calmer, more resilient life.

In these pages, you'll meet people who are facing the problems most commonly reported in our Busy as F*ck worlds. Some will resonate with you – or you'll spot traits of people you know. Whenever you get an 'aha' moment, you'll find tips, tools and tactics to guide your own journey. Here we go then; let the first session begin.

We Say Hello

Come on in, Busy As F*ck person.

Thanks for inviting me into your world – or at least picking up this book. I know you have a million other demands on your time so I'm aware of how lucky I am to get a sniff of it.

The first thing I do when I meet someone new is to make them feel comfortable. This may sound obvious but when people reach out for help – nervous, excited, agitated, tearful, hopeful and occasionally carrying more baggage than an ocean liner – they need warmth and reassurance. They need to know I'm fully in their corner. It also helps to look okay: not too stern or whispery or wearing really bad shoes.

My other aim is to stay neutral, to avoid making assumptions about you or your story. Again, that sounds easy but it can be a challenge because we all carry biases borne of our own history, experiences and beliefs. From the moment any of us meet another, a bubble forms in our heads. *Who? What? Wow! Are you serious? Why would you say that? Why would you DO that??* An intelligent young woman once accused me of judging her. When I protested, she raised her hand in my face. 'You'd better be judging me because I'm paying you to figure me out. Besides, I'm judging you.' She was eyeballing my scuffed ankle boots as she said this and it flashed through my mind that I'd made a poor fashion choice that morning.

Thrown slightly, I didn't know what to say. 'How am I doing so far?' I half-stammered, setting myself up.

'Keep trying,' she said. 'Jury's still out.'

The jury stayed out too, but she made a good point. We all constantly form opinions of each other – good and bad, high and low, helpful and destructive – but if I'm going to help you, I need to keep mine out of the way. People are full of surprises, complexities and contradictions, which is what makes the job so intriguing and, sometimes, so difficult. The stories you hear don't run in straight lines, either – not many people set out to lie but their versions of the truth may differ wildly from those of other people in their world, even from reality.

I was reminded of this when browsing through a book of famous news photographs. There was a stark black-and-white picture of a military husband returning from a Vietnam prisoner of war camp, his wife and kids joyous as they ran across the airport

15

tarmac towards him. The photo was a study in time, famous all over the world for capturing joy in the moment, the reuniting of a family, the euphoric ending to war.

But their story was less black and white. It turned out that the wife had written to her husband just days before his return saying she wanted a divorce. The marriage had reportedly been rocky when he left for Vietnam and she'd been with another man in his absence. But she was there, smiling on the tarmac, and her 'falseness' was proclaimed to the world (especially by her furious war-vet husband). I thought she was harshly judged: it's possible to be happy and sad at the same time. It is also true to say that the face we show to the world is not always an accurate window to our reality.

Nothing is as it seems. People are extremely skilled at concealing parts of themselves, sometimes for manipulative reasons, sometimes out of necessity – or fear.

I have seen kindergarten mums who moonlight as sex workers, exhausted by the twin demands of having sex with strangers and arranging play dates for their toddlers. I've met frail old ladies who once beat their sons with gas pipes yet expect these now strapping men to come over on Sundays and make them a cup of tea. I've known a brilliant maths teacher to have a laptop full of kiddie porn. Wonderful, warm parents whose own parents left them home alone or in the car outside the pub while they drank and shot up drugs every night; a successful business executive with a cocaine habit (make that more than one); a chief executive who lived alone and couldn't take a housemate because she needed to throw up her meal every evening; a stoic police officer who hid the bruises and scratches inflicted by his alcoholic, personality-disordered wife under his uniform; a star athlete who dated every woman in sight (briefly) because he was terrified of being outed as gay.

16

People cry when they're happy, smile when they're in pain, and willingly have sex with people they hate. I've known socially anxious people to cheat on their partners when they barely have the confidence to say hello to someone. How does that happen?

So when we meet, I assume nothing, even if I'm privy to some part of your story. The challenge for me is to wipe out all I know and start with the blankest slate, just to open the door and welcome you in.

Show-and-Tell Time

'How can I help you?' I'll ask, to kick things off.

Most are ready for this question. They've overthought it carefully; they have a shopping list of difficulties, but it can still be challenging to lay it all out in a coherent, ordered way. Some people have made notes on their phones, tablets or scraps of paper; others just allow all that has been spinning in their heads for weeks and months to tumble forth. Some open their mouths to speak and nothing comes out. It's not that they don't have anything to say – more that they have too much. Being Busy as F*ck generally means your mind is jammed to capacity, with all you have to do, with worries about past, present and future. So we need to take it slowly. If we try to download too much information at the outset, it can feel like an avalanche. And that's not helpful for either of us.

Some people are churned up with worry because feeling off their game mentally is new ground for them. They understand problems with the body but the mind is a whole new arena. So the question burning underneath is, '*What's wrong with me?*' or '*Is there something REALLY wrong with me?*'

While there can be serious issues, in most cases people are feeling stuck, overwhelmed or lost – or they've been experiencing foreign thoughts, emotions and behaviours. Occasionally, they are convinced they have symptoms they've read about or seen on a TV medical drama, which featured someone behaving out-of-the-box crazy or with the rarest (and unlikely) hybrid of clinical disorders.

Making people feel normal with whatever's going on for them is a thread that runs the entire length of our work. I thought this was common to all health professionals until my friend told me about her visit to the dentist. She had, for a reason unknown to her, produced excess saliva and was horribly embarrassed. The dentist didn't mask his shock: 'Wow. I've never seen anything like it. I believe there are special waterproof aprons for this,' he said, describing the oral health version of a wetsuit. 'I'll try to get one in for next time.'

'He made me feel like a pipe had burst,' she said.

'Had it? I mean, was it like a river?' I asked, as we collapsed with laughter.

There wasn't a next time for this dentist. Just saying. But I don't want to contribute to a generalised fear of dentistry. It was just a useful reminder of the importance of normalising *all* problems. Imagine if I said to someone having panic attacks, 'OMG, I've never been here before. You are the most anxious person I've *ever* seen. I believe someone in the Antarctic has developed an ice tank for this; I'll get one shipped for our next appointment.' While it's possible this person will feel special, they'll also walk out the door a whole lot more worried than when they came in.

Psychology, a bit like dentistry, has a hard enough job selling itself. There are still people who believe you have to be insane or delusional or falling into a gutter or slipping in and out of multiple personalities to see a therapist – and it's our duty to keep chopping that tree down.

For a few years after I qualified, my own mum would say, 'You'll never run out of work. There are too many nutty people out there.'

And I'd smile and say the same thing every time. 'Not nutty. Just people, people just like you and me who are having problems.'

She stopped saying it after a while and, gradually, thankfully, more people are joining her.

More people are opening up about their struggles, which is both healthy and a positive shift for mental health. But there is a long way to go before the stigma, the old-school thinking, is permanently pushed aside. There is a marathon to run before prejudice around mental health issues is eradicated.

The World According to You

What's up? What's Going On In Your World?

That's the first thing we need to consider in mapping out a plan for you. We need to understand how your own brand of Busy as F*ck is affecting the way you think, feel and behave – and, more broadly, its impact on your life.

Of course, Busy as F*ck can be a good, even great, thing. There's a lot to do – and we can't sit around staring at it. We do need to smash the to-do list. We need to be #productive. We need to press forward. We need to use our time well. We need to succeed. We need to serve. We need to make our unique contribution to the world. Because if we don't, if we lie in bed with a supersize bag of crisps watching reality TV, it will be a life misspent. A life too ordinary. And imagine the horror of that.

Seriously though, being Busy as F*ck can aid our quest to build meaningful lives. It also has a whiff of cool; we all (secretly) want to be that person who achieves great things: who's a hot-shot at work, runs their home like a domestic god or goddess, is an engaged partner, loving parent *and* who never forgets to pick up milk on the way home. The challenge is to keep Busy as F*ck in check, to know when (and how) to pull back and to be able to sit on the deck sipping wine without doubt, guilt and fear joining us. If we are going to squeeze the most from ourselves and our all-too-short lives, we need to be able to gauge when our Busy as F*ckness is compromising (or drip-feed destroying) our physical and emotional health, when we're hurting people we love, when we're becoming that person others want to hide from.

But where do we start? How do we know?

Check Yourself Out (but Not in a Mirror)

It's an unwritten rule of psychology that before getting down to work, you need a vice-like grip on the problem. I'd go even further: to not fully understand what's going on for someone is to invite trouble over, sit it down and make it a coffee.

In the first session, there are four things we need to know:

1. How Busy (and content) are you?
2. Where is Busy biting you (and where isn't it)?
3. How can you tell when Busy is too much?
4. Does your personality style make you vulnerable to Busy?

1. How Busy (and Content) Are You?

I know, small book, big question. But what's going on in your life – and your view of it – is critical information. People are not islands. Our relationships, families, work, kids, bodies, health, finances and home environments can all influence our life satisfaction – as well as our busyness.

Traditionally, therapy (and coaching too) focuses on the tough stuff, what's going wrong for you: how bad your sleeping or nutrition is, how your body is reacting to stress, how much your mind is turning in on itself, how painful your relationships or work situation are – all the reasons that prompted you to reach out for help. While all that's important, we also need to square it off against what's going right.

A more helpful starting point is to check in on your life satisfaction. After all, if you're Busy as F*ck and that's the life for you, then no-one has any right to drag you out of it. However, I suspect if you're reading this, then you're in some way up for change or adding new skills – or at least helping others you care about do the same.

Boohoo Versus Woohoo: Rate Your Life Satisfaction

Put a slash mark (with a pen or in your mind) where you rate your satisfaction with your life right now. Not happiness – we're not going there (yet), just your general level of contentment. A rating of 10 obviously means you're sublimely happy; 1 means you're in a pit of despair.

My life is …

1 (boohoo) — — — — — — — — — — 10 (woohoo)

How do you rate? Are you okay with that? Can you live with it? Could it be better?

Now think about how much that rating has changed over time. How would you have rated a year ago? Five years ago?

Why?

Any changes are usually deeply related to your circumstances. If there is a marked change, it is important to be honest with yourself about the reason. Maybe you have a new partner (or you've lost one), moved to a new town or country, lost your job or scored a great new one, been devastated by natural disaster or won lotto. If your rating has moved up the scale, identify what's going right (and why) – and how you can create more of it. Seriously, we don't spend enough time thinking about *what is good in our lives and what we are good at*, which would hugely help our resilience.

If your rating has taken a negative slide, whether there's a clear reason for it or not, there are plenty of tools in this book to help.

Rate Your Busy as F*ck Self

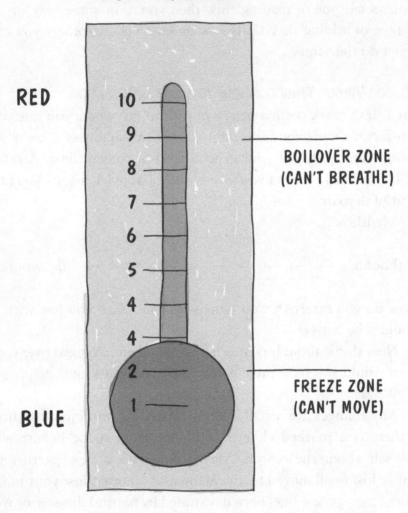

BAF RATING

RED

10
9
8
7
6
5
4
4
2
1

BLUE

BOILOVER ZONE
(CAN'T BREATHE)

FREEZE ZONE
(CAN'T MOVE)

Again, mark your own busyness levels – now and in your ideal world. Go with what you are feeling right now. Obviously 'can't move' and 'can't breathe' are metaphors for completely detached from life and running yourself ragged – but you know what I mean.

Results

Psychology is not about absolutes, so there are no right and wrong answers to this exercise. We're a 'Shades of Grey' profession, so to speak. But the aim is to get you thinking about the *gap* between *how busy you're feeling right now* and *how you would like to feel*.

Ratings are obviously a personal thing. Extreme scores – either way – worry me, but it's not my life. If you score yourself 10/10 for busyness, and that's the way you like and want things, that's fine (unless you are hurting your health or the people you care about). Same thing if you score 1/1 for completely disengaged and don't want to do more than that (and no-one you care about minds and your health hasn't bailed on you).

Ideally, you should aim for the place where you're at your peak for achievement and enjoyment but are not tipping into the out-of-control zone (too often), nor shutting yourself down completely.

Here is a basic guide to your scores, which applies to both your current and ideal busyness states:

9–10: You're probably too wired and need to think about reducing your Busy as F*ck levels right away. Even if you're a high achiever your stress levels will be undermining your capacity to think clearly, relax and have fun – and even to achieve to your peak.

7–8: Ideal as long as you can stay in this zone. Most of us can't; when things are going well we add more to the mix and – suddenly – we're in trouble. A little pressure is helpful, though, and can push us to peak performance, so don't be afraid to wind the dial up sometimes. Just make sure you get some downtime to balance it.

4–6: You're laid back, which is good – and helpful. But take an honest look at your life. Are you bored? Lost?

Unfulfilled? If you are perfectly at peace, that's great. But this score indicates there may be something missing. Perhaps it's time to find out what it is.

0–3: Time to make your move – on life, the universe, everything. And hurry up or you'll be old before your time. Extreme disengagement is as bad for you as extreme tension. And it will trigger and maintain a whole lot of bad habits.

What to do: If there's a yawning gap between where you are and where you want to be, let's do something about it. Come up with one thing you could do right now to move your rating in your ideal direction. It doesn't have to be life-changing, just something you could do *today* or *this week* that indicates a tiny change. Then resolve to *do* it. The world is (too) full of good intent.

2. Where Is Busy Biting You (and Where Isn't It)?

We've been fed a lot of lies about busyness. Perhaps the biggest of them is, 'If you want something done, ask a busy person'. The logic goes like this: if you are already juggling six balls, it's pretty easy to add a seventh. That may be true, but when you eventually drop a ball (and you will) you risk all the others going down with it – and it becomes an immense task to pick them up again.

How much we can do, carry or fit in depends on our individual capacities, as well as whether our health can sustain it. The trick is to find your own sweet spot, to figure out how you can live as fully as possible without going crazy.

There's no blueprint for Busy as F*ck. It can show up in many ways: through emotions, thoughts, physiological symptoms and/ or behaviours – usually it's a combination of them all.

Sometimes Busy as F*ck feels as if you're just going through the motions or you're running on a treadmill with the incline and speed wound slightly too high, racing between obligations and tasks, never quite nailing the to-do list. And, at the end of every day, you quietly wonder, *Is this it? Is this really my life? Do I have to do it all again tomorrow? CAN I do it? Where will it end?*

It can show up physiologically, with headaches, heart palpitations, sweaty palms, tingling muscles, extreme fatigue, colds and flus that keep coming, shallow breathing or just that rolling unease in your stomach. You can deal with it, and you don't tell anyone, but you wish it wasn't there. You worry no-one else feels this way, but you shouldn't, because they do: they're just hiding it as well as you are.

Busy as F*ck can also hijack your thoughts, so you never get a moment's peace. While you may look chilled and cheerful on the outside, your head is buzzing with unwanted thoughts – racing, intrusive and negative. Or you're worrying excessively, overthinking events and interactions to exhaustion, so you can't find space in your whirring brain for anything else. *Did I do the right thing? Did I say the wrong thing? Does she even like me? Why didn't he text me back? Was that post stupid? What if people think I'm boring?* And on it goes – a never-ending loop of worry.

As well, Busy as F*ck can show up in our behaviours. When we feel overwhelmed we may withdraw, or isolate ourselves from family and friends. Extreme busyness can seep into our close relationships (*Are you even listening to me? Can you put that bloody phone away for once?*) and our work (*I'm too busy to talk to you right now; can you send me an email about that?*) Our moods and emotions can dip and swing: we can be unreasonably irritable or lash out unfairly at people we love (often over quite trivial things). Or we can mistreat or neglect our bodies through exercise, food, alcohol and other substances. And, of course, Busy as F*ck can morph into serious mental health problems, such as depression, various anxieties, addictions and, at the sharpest, and most tragic end, suicide.

When Busy spins out of control, some people shout and scream, some quake and shake, some are stoic and silent, some confront, some stonewall, some avoid everyone and everything. Some notice they feel a little 'off' but they carry on, hoping it will sort itself out. Others don't notice, or ignore the warning signs, allowing themselves to get seriously unwell before speaking up or seeking help. That can be because they want to be 'tough' or don't want to admit they are struggling or simply that they don't want to crack open the dam in case they start a flood. While I'm all for being resolute, for tapping into your internal resources, it can be scary when people hold on too long. It's better to understand how stress hurts you and when it's starting to slam into your quality of life.

The Stress Monster

We're all managing stress – it's a rare person who is stress-free. I'm not sure I've seen one. But stress in even one key area of your life can take a hefty toll. And when it bombards from all directions, it can eat you up physically, mentally and emotionally.

So what are the key areas? We've all seen those checklists that ask you to add up the stress factors in your life, ranging from the heavy hitters (death, separation or divorce, serious illness, financial loss, redundancy, retirement, pregnancy, moving countries) through to issues we might be having with our work, families or children – and whose place to go to for Christmas (actually a nightmare for some).

While these tests are fun and validating (*Wow, I've got 300 stress points; no wonder I feel terrible*), they can be a wildly inaccurate measure of how, and how much, they're impacting you, simply because the meaning we each attach to stress factors varies, and the way we handle difficulty depends on many factors, including our own resilience and support networks.

When we're overwhelmed, it's easy to 'globalise' negative feelings – to tell ourselves that *everything* is bad, even when it's not. So it's helpful to identify our key stress points so we know where to begin in addressing them – and to separate them from what is good in your world.

So try this. Grab some sticky notes and, using the Life Events checklist below as a guide, write down your main stress factors. Then rank them in order (most stressful to least). Maybe this was obvious to you – but it's surprising how often it's not. This will show you precisely what's going on, what your top priority is and whether you can control it (or not). When you have identified No. 1, ask yourself if this is something you can do something proactive about. If so, come up with something (even tiny) you can do to bring your stress down. This will help give you some ownership of what is going on and send your brain the message that you are 'doing something' about it. (If you have no control over whatever is going on, move to No. 2 on the list and repeat the process.)

When you've done that, take a moment to identify the areas that are thriving or going well for you, because it will provide balance. Take your time. Life can feel smothering when we're highly stressed but there are always things to celebrate and be grateful for, however small. Sometimes we need to push ourselves to look for them.

Life events checklist

- ❑ Work (too much, too little, none, workplace drama, bullying, unsatisfying work)
- ❑ Intimate relationships (sex, lies, love, loneliness and the whole raft of relationship drama)
- ❑ Family issues (conflicts, blended families, solo and step parenting, ageing parents, not having a family)
- ❑ Kids (our worries about our children are an arena all of their own)
- ❑ Alcohol and drugs; addictions and abuse

❏ Social issues (social anxiety, friendship problems, moving country/city/town, isolation and loneliness, ageing)

❏ Gender and sexuality (uncertainty, secrets, transitions)

❏ Money (poverty or debt or too much drain on financial resources; I've only ever seen one person who was struggling with too much money – winning Lotto can be a curse, too, although that's hard for most of us to accept)

❏ Study (can't cope, poor marks, falling behind, perfectionist standards)

❏ Health (sickness, disability, surgery, physical and mental problems, caregiving)

❏ Time (mostly not having enough time. Few – if any – complain of the luxury of time, having too much time for themselves or to pursue their interests)

❏ Weight, body image and food issues (way more troubling to people than those who don't have these issues might expect)

3. How Can You Tell When Busy Is Too Much?

As a clinical psychologist, I'm often assessing for serious mental health issues. Even though Busy as F*ck can impact our health, it's not a clinical problem. That's because stress is hard to quantify. Psychologically, it's better described as a range of symptoms that can develop into depression, anxiety or other serious issues.

Of the serious fallouts of Busy as F*ck lifestyles, depression (characterised by low mood) and anxiety (characterised by fear and worry) are the most common – and they tend to stick together. It makes sense: if you are feeling down, you worry about it, and if you are worried, it drags your mood down. While it's possible to be anxious without being depressed, I can't recall a case of depression that didn't have anxiety riding shotgun. Fear loves company.

The point where busy meets anxiety should be red-stickered, though, because while Busy as F*ck may work for you, Anxious as F*ck will not. The term 'anxiety' is often used interchangeably with worry and stress but clinical anxiety is another level altogether – it can turn you inside out, frazzling your nerves, draining your energy and scarily detaching you from your people and your world. After a while you'll worry not just about all you have to do, but your sanity as well. You'll worry about your worrying. You'll scan your body for problems. Chaotic feelings can become your new norm, as well as your biggest worry, and that can be a difficult cycle to break.

People are now relatively educated in mental health, due to the vast reams of information available online. While Doctor Google has its critics, it's helped to tear away some of the mystery around mental health and psychological problems. Online tests for depression and anxiety, food and alcohol problems and other conditions can help you make sense of how you are feeling, thinking and behaving. They can also press your panic buttons: *yes, I have that. AND that. AND that. OMG, what's going on?*

If you score highly on these online tests, especially if you have suicidal thoughts, you should see your GP or a clinical professional for an assessment. But otherwise, online tests can be a useful starting point. What they don't do, though, is consider you as an individual, a living, breathing human. They don't take in the context of your life or your people; they don't assess your strengths, they don't map the results onto you as a person, which is not helpful because that's what makes all the difference to your resilience and ability to cope.

In order to treat a person effectively for any mental illness, you need a broad picture of who they are, how they think and function, and who's in their world. You might be able to lift off some of their acute symptoms without it, but you won't get the kind of sustained good outcome possible if you are able to pull

together all the available information about who they are in the world.

So, by all means, jump online and do the tests – but be aware of their limits. The most important thing to note is any *change* in your *capacity to function* and your *quality of life*.

Red Flags

So when should we take note? Red flags, or symptoms, are the earliest signs of stress overload and tend to overlap with depression and anxiety. We all experience some of these from time to time, so there's no need to panic. But if you're experiencing clusters, say five or more, and they haven't begun to lift after several weeks, don't bury your head in the proverbial sand. Acknowledging a problem is the first step in coming back from it.

- Changes in eating, exercise habits
- Body changes (weight increase, decrease or notable fluctuations)
- Physical health problems (headaches, stomach aches, frequent colds and flus, unexplained aches and pains)
- Wakeful or disrupted sleep; always feeling fatigued on waking
- Irritability and lack of tolerance
- Overthinking: racing thoughts or ruminating on a problem
- Relationship problems
- Increased use of alcohol, cigarettes or substances
- Extreme fatigue
- Low motivation and energy; feeling flat
- Extreme agitation and restlessness
- Concentration, focus and decision-making problems
- Excessive worry in one or more areas of your life (especially if you can tell this is more than necessary for whatever is going on)

- Being overwhelmed, feeling you'll never get on top of things
- Struggle to get pleasure or fun from things you once enjoyed
- Withdrawal from people and activities

The Perfect Storm

Beware the perfect storm, I always say to my clients. Or if I don't say it, I'm thinking it and I'm scouting for the signs it's blowing their way.

The perfect storm is the eye of the stress, like the movie of the same name, where all the forces of nature (or life) smash together at the same time. I'm often amazed how much stress people can handle, how brilliantly they can step up in a crisis, even when they didn't appear to be emotionally robust. They may crash later, of course, but at the time people can hold a boatload of pain and act bravely in the face of it.

I've worked with many people exposed to trauma in their work– police and firefighters, criminal defence lawyers, doctors, hospital emergency and ambulance workers and coronial staff – who live and breathe death. While they might model resilience at work, the crash can come when something also goes wrong at home – especially if they were already emotionally vulnerable.

A relationship breakdown on the back of long hours, a heavy workload or workplace difficulties is one of the most common flashpoints.

I saw a police officer, a young father, who had attended seven sudden deaths over two months. He was first responder in most of them, including a horrific dead-baby case. He was sent for a psychological appointment to make sure he was fit for work – and he was – until he heard a rumour his partner was cheating. She wasn't – it was idle gossip – but the strain of recent months blew out, nightmares about death escalated and he needed a significant amount of time off work.

Five Questions to Ask Yourself

Here are the additional questions I use to assess when things are heading down a more serious track. (Note: they don't include safety questions for suicide risk – if you have these you should see a professional.)

* Have your activity/presentation levels dropped?

Take an honest look at what you do with your weekends. Weekends are a better gauge than weekdays because they lack the structure of a working week. That makes it easier to spot a change. Are your activity levels the same or similar as previously? Are they as enjoyable or a shadow of their former selves? Do you end the weekends having 'not done much' other than try to rest/relax? Take particular notice if you have stopped putting effort into what you wear and (even slightly) let go your hygiene and presentation standards.

* Are you having fun?

When you're struggling mentally your mood becomes heavier and your sense of humour can go into hiding. Check if your laughter is still genuine and light, against whether you feel you are just chugging through the motions. I've been met with a lot of blank stares in response to this question: ask yourself when was the last time you genuinely had fun – the answer may surprise you.

* Are you avoiding things?

Do you find yourself regularly saying 'no' to things (or people) you used to enjoy – and not in a healthy way? Have you started to shut down socially? Do you find yourself retreating from activities and invitations rather than stepping forward? Do you feel like you're stuck – especially in more than one area of your life?

* Have you felt your personality shift?

Do you feel less of a person or a less interesting person than you used to be? Have you lost your spark? Your confidence? Your creativity? This is an interesting one to run past people close to you – they often notice any change before you do.

* Have taking a break/holiday and/or your usual relaxation strategies stopped working?

Have you rolled out all the things that normally relax and refresh you and felt no difference? Take particular note if you don't feel refreshed after a holiday (or if it doesn't last more than a day or two) because it should.

Results

Your answers are no reason to panic – but if a pattern is setting in you may need to check in with those who know you well to gauge their thoughts, and/or a professional to assess what's going on. What is certain, though, is you need to make a change. Doing more of the same will get you – surprise, surprise – more of the same. Is that what you really want?

When to Talk, When to Act

When you are struggling you may have thoughts of suicide. These can be fleeting or sustained – and often people keep functioning very well alongside them.

If you have thoughts of wanting to die, it's important to speak up: talking is a healthy first step. And if someone close to you says they are feeling this way you should listen, empathise, reassure them of their reasons for living and encourage healthy behaviours. You should also let them know you will be telling someone who can share the responsibility and/or help professionally. You should not try, or be expected, to keep someone's suicidal thoughts a 'secret'. So tell someone.

Suicide is sometimes, sadly, a very real consequence of mental health struggles. While we can note the risk factors, there are no guaranteed predictors. Suicide raises, and leaves behind, many questions, which loved ones should not be expected, or force themselves, to answer. The suffering can be immense and those touched by it deserve our understanding and support.

4. Does Your Personality Style Make You Vulnerable to Busy?

We each turn up in the world with our own family history, stories, our own set of birth circumstances, but who *we* are and how *we* function influences how *we* manage Busy as F*ck lifestyles.

People who cope well tend to share certain personality traits or skills, such as resilience, intuition, empathy, emotional regulation, creativity and adaptability. Other characteristics can increase vulnerability, especially when life is a crazy rush.

Six personality styles are arguably the most vulnerable when life spills into the Busy as F*ck zone and anxiety levels soar. There's considerable overlap between the styles. While you may relate heavily to one or two categories, you may spot a little of yourself in others.

The Perfectionist
Meme: *'Get it right or go home.'*
Features: Unrealistically high expectations of themselves, others and life generally: nothing is ever quite good enough. In relentlessly pursuing high standards, you feel things could always be better so it means you get little rest, which can be tough on your health when life is already frantic. Because you tend to focus on your flaws and mistakes, you often dismiss or downplay your achievements. You may suffer from creative paralysis because

you'd rather do nothing than risk imperfection or falling short of expectations.

Highest need: Learn when to stop; acknowledge your achievements (instead of your faults).

The Competitor

Meme: *'I'm okay if I'm doing better than you.'*

Features: The Competitor has usually done well in a particular field and been widely recognised, and rewarded, for it. Competitors rate themselves by comparing achievements with others and on tangible things, such as scores or grades (or houses, cars, trophy partners or even your kids' achievements). Because you've enjoyed a lot of success, that style has worked well for you. But you live with insecurity and a secret fear of failing because that's not something you have experienced often, or understand. When you get overwhelmed, criticised or have a setback, you take it hard, and may struggle to cope and find your way back.

Highest Need: Understanding of yourself outside your chosen field. Learn to measure yourself as a person, not by what you have, what you've done or who you're with.

The Denialist

Meme: *'Just keep going – no matter what.'*

Features: The Denialist isn't aware of, or tends to ignore, the clear signs of stress overload, even physical symptoms like extreme fatigue, headaches and nervous stomachs. That means you will keep pushing yourself without taking time out or slowing down, possibly until you hit exhaustion point – or you get sick. While your energy and efficiency is admirable, you find it hard to relax, which is taxing on you – and those who love you. When you try to slow down your head fills with things you *should* or *could* be doing and the guilt that goes with it. You have a history of overextending (trying to squeeze too much into the time available), which often leads you to sacrifice your own needs and self-care, such as exercise, time out, social time.

Highest need: Relaxation and calming skills. Plan (and take) time for yourself.

The Controller

Meme: *'I can't cope with change.'*

Features: The Controller wants everything in life to be predictable – and when it's not (which is often in our Busy as F*ck worlds) the struggle begins and the anxiety escalates. At home and work, you thrive with order and routines, and you tend to be a good organiser. But change of any kind, and the uncertainty that brings, winds you up and you'll fear the worst possible outcome. This causes you to focus excessively on finding a solution in order to restore a feeling of calm. The trouble is, you never feel entirely calm. Trusting in life's processes, and managing its twists and turns, is extremely challenging for you.

Highest need: Learn to tolerate uncertainty. Challenge and reframe your thinking to see that change could be a good thing.

The Pleaser

Meme: *'I need you to like me. Please.'*

Features: The Pleaser needs a steady stream of validation from other people in order to feel okay in the world. Most of your actions are underpinned by wanting to be noticed, approved of or loved. You're often a kind, do-anything-for-anyone person and you constantly get asked for favours because there's a higher-than-most chance you'll say yes. You often worry that you haven't done enough at work or at home or for others, or think about what else you could do for them – and then do it – but it causes resentment when you realise how little you are getting in return. In trying to please everyone in a Busy as F*ck world you can stagger under the ever-increasing load.

Highest need: Learn to say no and to take no without being hurt. Invest in yourself and boost self-esteem so you can get the approval you need from yourself.

The Chameleon

Meme: *'Keeping up appearances.'*

Features: There's a little of the Chameleon in all of us – none of our social media posts reveal our Full Authentic Selves because, well, that might be a little scary. But I've included the Chameleon here because people who consistently mask themselves from others, or morph into various personas depending on who they are with and what's happening, tend to carry a deep insecurity about who they are in the world. Sometimes Chameleons have a dark agenda, but frequently you're just desperately trying to cope with insecurities, uncertainty, feeling out of control and trying to find your place. Constantly 'reading the room' and adapting yourself to fit in with others can be exhausting, though, so your self-care needs monitoring.

Highest need: Learn to drop the mask – at least with people you trust. Build a fuller sense of yourself – what you enjoy, what you're good at, who you like to be with.

Where Do You Fit?

If you spotted traits in yourself, hold that thought. Self-understanding is part of the secret to coping, and thriving, in a Busy as F*ck world, but it's what you do with the knowledge that makes the biggest difference.

In the next session we dig a little deeper into your personality and how you function in the world. Ready? Let's delve.

Who Are You?

My phone rings late one evening. It's a sports manager I know: one of the players is having a meltdown on the eve of an international. Could I come to their hotel and sort him out?

The manager sounds wound tight, worried. The player, Bryn, is one of the most experienced on the team, but today at training he abruptly left the field, saying he was having trouble breathing. Back at the hotel he retreated to his room, refused to come out for dinner and was begging to be withdrawn from the next day's match.

'He's saying he's lost his feel for the game. His confidence is shot and this is the very worst time for this to happen,' the manager says.

I hesitate. I don't want to foster an 'ambulance at the bottom of the cliff' culture but this is one of my first big jobs in sport and I'm eager to do the right thing. I agree to go, if only to calm him down. That's the thing about mental health problems – they scare people.

I find Bryn alone in his hotel room, sitting with his head between his knees, staring at the floor. I introduce myself and when he looks up, his forehead is unnaturally lined, his face a waxy grey. His eyes are bloodshot and I suspect he's been crying. He sweeps a long strand of hair out of his eyes.

'There's something wrong with me,' he says. 'I can't go out there anymore. I can't play.'

I sit down next to him, trying to look calm and capable, but I'm not sure what to do. I'm in a hotel room with a young man, a stranger. I know a little about him from the news media but have no personal information and I'm charged with making him feel safe, calming his panic and getting him on the field within 24 hours. Not just standing out there either – playing well enough to do himself, his team and his nation proud. It's a very big ask, for both of us.

It's also precarious: research tells us that what makes psychology most effective is the relationship between the two parties. But it's hard to build that bridge when the person in front of you is in a high state of distress. Athletes – anyone, actually – can be reluctant to open up to someone who's been forced on them, no matter how qualified that person. Trust doesn't fall out of the sky.

He looks across at me briefly, then back at the floor. Then – suddenly– he stands up and stalks across the room to his sports bag. He pulls out a commemorative cap and slams it on his head. It's too small and he looks like an overgrown schoolboy. Then he takes it off and flings it across the room. 'I worked for this since I was a young boy. Now I don't want to do it. I can't do it. You know what …'

Now he's standing over me, his voice loud, almost shrill. 'This is not my dream anymore. It's everybody else's. I'm not playing for me. I haven't been for a long time.'

I don't say anything, just sit there, my eyes on the wall. Forced eye contact is a barrier we don't need. Young men often find it difficult to express themselves, to find words to match their feelings. Talking about emotions can be foreign, even threatening, ground. But he is eager to talk, even with his thoughts tangled like Spaghetti Junction.

He tells me about his career, from age six when he first showed uncanny hand-eye co-ordination. From there he became Bryn the Athlete, the boy who was good at every sport he touched, who made all the top teams, who got all the girls, was pampered by his family, who the teachers let get away with not doing any homework. Cushioned by his talent, he'd grown up being told how wonderful he was, that he was destined for greatness and all the trappings that went with it. Bryn's parents had not reinforced other skills or interests, not because they were bad parents, just because they hadn't needed to: his path was laid out. They had never intentionally traded off his sporting prowess, but people were always asking about him and they were happy to talk: your child's success is an easy topic.

I have heard this story many times, in many different settings, each with a slightly different spin. The main character is always a child with remarkable ability in sports, music, academia or the arts. Their lives are mapped out for them because of their talent. They are nurtured and fawned over. Everything they touch turns golden; very little goes wrong for them.

For athletes, if the professional scouts come calling it can be a heady cocktail – huge money, sex, travel, drugs, gambling and all manner of temptations. But when they are 28, carrying chronic injuries, or had one head knock too many, they can find themselves in a pit of despair because sport is all they know. Retirement is a difficult time for those who have built a life around athletic talent but have to redefine themselves when they're barely 30.

While they are on the rise, things are easy – but their identity is built solely on their talent. Success, combined with all the attention, creates an overblown sense of self-esteem, a False Ego. Outwardly they brim with confidence but that often masks intense self-doubt. When they strike real difficulty they plunge mentally as they are simply not equipped to deal with tough times. They do not have the tools or resilience to pick up again. Mental toughness, or the ability to 'bounce back', comes from the School of Hard Knocks – and that's not one you can pay to attend.

The fallout: they become frightened to perform in case they fail. Because failure will mean they are nothing.

That's where Bryn was. On the back of some inconsistent form, media debate about his selection and heavy social media criticism, his future was for the first time uncertain.

The problem wasn't his sport or his talent: it was that he had no idea who he was without it.

So let's turn to you.

We Talk About You

Once we've drawn up a picture of what's going on in your life – the good, the bad and the Busy as F*ck factor – it's time to delve into the self. This is the fun stuff (for both of us) because getting to know yourself is the essence of psychology.

In Bryn's case, we had to deal with what was in front of us first. You can't tap straight to a person's core when they are struggling to breathe – let alone function. It was a matter of putting some anxiety management strategies in place to help him quickly back on the field – and he was able to do so, even perform adequately. Beyond that, though, he needed help to understand what was going on for him and insight into who he was as a man – not just an athlete. He needed to learn ways to measure himself that did not involve statistics or other men.

Like Bryn, all of us are people first. The other roles we take on or perform (such as mother, brother, son, aunty, farmer, doctor, office worker, friend, athlete, student, nephew) are subsets of the people we are. That may sound obvious, but in a Busy as F*ck world we can get so caught up in our various roles and day-to-day duties that we don't have, or form, a larger view of ourselves or what we stand for – which is what gives us a strong foothold in the world. One of the most common things you hear when people are struggling is, 'I don't know who I am' or 'I've never really known who I am.' So that's the number one goal in pursuit of building a meaningful life: getting to know who you are.

***

'Be yourself', is an instruction we've all heard, over and over and over. Until we really don't need to hear that anymore.

We all get the theory: our uniqueness is what we bring to the world, we shouldn't compare ourselves with others, no-one can 'do us' better than we can. But when you don't yet know who you are, how do you go about being yourself?

And, even if you know, dare you risk revealing your true self when the thing you want most in the world (especially if you are under 20) is to fit in.

The drive to fit in begins early. Some experts say babies learn quickly what a gummy smile does for their approval rating, but the social forces of the world turn up the heat in middle childhood. First comes self-awareness on trainer wheels, then we begin to position ourselves in relation to others. Am I prettier than her? Better at football? Or reading? Darker or lighter? Taller? Fatter? Stronger? Faster?

By the time we hit our teens, all this has blown into a desperate desire to find our place and our people. It's why adolescents so frequently report feeling lost and low as they attempt to make connections, bouncing between the opposing needs of dependence on their parents and freedom with their peers. Not being able to bridge that gap can be hugely distressing. It's also very normal. Who among us, looking back, can say, 'I so had my sh*t together at 14; I'd found my tribe for life'. Virtually no-one.

But kids don't understand that practically everyone they know is going through the same thing, so the phase can be agonising. And when you're deep in adolescent despair it's not helpful to be told all will be well.

Once I saw a 23-year-old woman in the grips of a life-threatening eating disorder. Her mother, who was loving and hugely supportive, kept telling her daughter she'd be okay because she had 'so much potential'.

While her words were well meaning they made the young woman feel worse about her struggle, widening the gap between where she was and what all her friends were doing. Her mother wisely came to remove 'potential' from her vocab. While the young woman needed to set small goals, it was also important to make her feel 'good enough' just as she was, in the space she was in.

Generation Selfie

People are fascinated with, and by, themselves – I say that kindly – and although Generation Selfie takes the heat for this, it's not a new phenomenon. We've always been supremely interested in ourselves; it's just that the 21st century, and smartphone culture, has given us cooler ways to show it.

Therapy has the jump on smartphones, though, as it offers the best excuse to get close to yourself without seeming weird. If you try to work on yourself at home ('I need a few hours away from you to get to know myself') you are likely to score some raised eyebrows. It's a whole lot easier to say you are going to the gym. People are okay with you building your body. But bench-pressing your mind? Hmmm, okaaaaay. Pass the remote.

So people are more than up for self-exploration. Some view it as a grand adventure, some as an experiment; others see themselves as a project, something to be 'worked on' or 'fixed', which always makes me a little nervous because personal development doesn't have a deadline. There's no such thing as closing the file on yourself with a grand flourish: that's it, I'm done. I'm good to go back out into the world as a bright, shiny magnet to all who cross my path.

But for all that self-interest, it still surprises me how little people understand about the way they function in the world. They can tell you detailed stories from their past and about their families, that their favourite colour is green, that they're a chips over cheesecake person and that their secret passion is snail farming. But ask them how they react to stress or criticism, or manage their emotions, or what makes their hearts thump or how other people see them, and there's often an awkward silence.

When you think about it, how would we know? We don't have Get to Know Yourself classes in school, which would be more useful than just about anything else. We rely, instead, on what the world throws at us, trying to make sense of it as we go along, which is scary because it can skew our self-perception wildly, inaccurately and sometimes even dangerously.

All too often what we know about ourselves is based on the feedback we've had from others, our families or frequently unreliable or mean people. It can come from one-liners scrawled on school reports by tired teachers (Lucy is disruptive; Oscar has no initiative; Maggie will never be a mathematician) or stinging remarks from sports coaches (you'd run faster if you lost weight; you're too heavy to be a dancer) or bullies in the school playground (fat cow, four-eyes, faggot). Later on, it can come from bosses and colleagues, or those treacherous 360-degree feedback loops in which we receive toilet roll–long lists of work-ons from people who don't even like us.

But, still, we are curious. We long to know more. And that quest for self-knowledge has fed right into the booming online tracking industry, which allows us, with a tap at our phone or wrist, to record how much we are eating, sleeping, stepping, working, spending, using time and anything else that can be monitored and measured.

Tracking devices and smartphone apps are useful tools because they are an easy way of gathering personal data, which can be used to improve health and change behaviour. But the downside is that they make us hyper-aware of what we are doing, which then makes us stressed out and self-critical about what we are *not* doing.

For some reason, too, we feel compelled to share these personal gems. All tracking devices should come with a warning label that says please don't share this information *unless someone requests it*. The fact that you got REM sleep between 1 am and 4 am and the rest of the night you tossed and turned is not magnetic, no matter how much enthusiasm you put into your delivery. So be careful who you share with – unless it's a friendship you no longer want.

I'm serious, though. We could solve half the world's problems (or at least our own) if we understood ourselves better and, more importantly, we liked who we are.

Here's the best way I know of unpacking that.

The Pizza of Life

'Who am I?' is the oldest question in the book – fun to ask and impossible to answer with certainty.

That's probably why therapy or coaching sessions always land here in some form or other. I've spent hours on this with clients, experimenting with ways of breaking down self-identity until we hit on a winning methodology – pizza.

I came up with this while working with athletes such as Bryn in the example above – I wanted a metaphor we could all understand. When it worked for Bryn and his mates, I began using it more broadly and found it resonated just as well with everyone, regardless of age, gender, culture or occupation. Even kids, with some minor adjustments, picked up the concept easily – and it stuck.

The reason it works so well is because no matter who we are or what we do, we all get pizza, even the rare few who don't like it. Pizza is a universal language.

The Pizza of Life: How Does it Work?

The Pizza of Life is the world's simplest way of understanding who you are and how you feel about yourself.

The Pizza of Life represents your identity as a person. Note that this is not about work–life balance, so don't think about how much time you spend on each of these areas. Instead, think about how you feel about yourself in each sphere of your life.

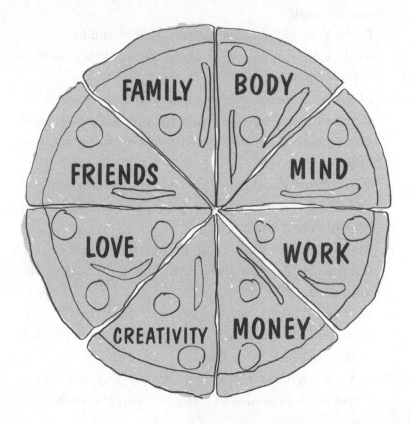

Divide your life into eight slices. Label each of them. When you have good, healthy self-identity it will look like this (below): you will feel equally good about yourself across all areas of your life. Before you start to worry, remember almost no-one has a perfectly formed pizza.

The headings used here are just a guideline. You can change them to suit yourself or your circumstances. You can also apply your own meanings to them. Here's a brief guide to those used here:

1. **Family.** The group of people *you* consider your family/whanau. This could be you and your partner, you and your child, your birth family, your extended family, your adopted family, the people who raised you or the group you live with.

2. **Body.** Your physical appearance, weight and fitness levels. Can include your clothing/the way you present in the world.

3. **Mind.** Your mental health, stress and anxiety levels, your resilience, emotional management and social skills. Can include spirituality or religious beliefs if those are important to you.

4. **Work.** What you do and how satisfied you are with it – and where it is likely to lead. Could also be about study, education and learning.

5. **Money.** Income, assets, cash in the bank. Whether you feel financially stable and able to fund the lifestyle you need/desire.

6. **Creativity.** Time to step outside your daily routine and create, invent and dream. The ability to stretch yourself in new and interesting ways.

7. **Love.** Intimate relationships or having people in your world you love (and who love you). This can look quite

different between people so identify who you have in your world and your satisfaction with them.

8. **Friends.** Your social circle. Who you spend time with (and how you feel after being with them). Some people seek out, and enjoy having, large social networks; for others, one or two close friends is fine.

When you have poor or out-of-whack self-identity it will look like this (below). It means you have too much invested in one particular area (e.g. work, your looks, your relationship, being a parent) to the detriment of others.

Very few people struggle in *all* areas, so it's important to look for the strengths as well as the vulnerabilities.

What's wrong with that? Well, nothing, as long as nothing ever goes wrong for you and your life never, ever changes. The trouble is, it will. Change will come and crap will happen. And when it strikes in your heavyweight area, the area loaded with your identity, the fall will really hurt.

When trouble smashes into Who We Are, it takes a greater toll. People struggle more mentally, and feel lost for far longer, when they have a narrow view of their self-worth. Having a broader sense helps cushion your landing and provides a foundation for your life.

Examples of big crashes:

- You are a successful corporate lawyer with a glowing track record. You've built your identity around that, and then work goes wrong: you get bullied, lose your job, get pushed sideways into a role you never wanted, or retire.

- You have always relied on your stunning good looks to win at life – get a partner, help your work prospects, be popular. Then you get older, gain weight, have children and begin to feel invisible. Take a double hit if how you look is connected to your work.

- You are a star athlete; you've won so many accolades and have legions of fans. You're reaching the peak of your powers when you suffer a career-ending injury. The end of your athletic life, as well as the speed it arrived, means you have to completely rebuild who you are.

- You are a dedicated wife and mother. You've raised three great kids and the last of them is just about to leave home. You find out your partner of 25 years is leaving you for someone younger. You feel suddenly not needed or valued – you have to start again.

What to Do?

Bite into the pizza to see if you're content with the spread of your self-identity. Ask these questions:

- Do I have too much of my self loaded on one slice?
- If something went wrong in my primary area, would I still feel good enough in other areas of my life?
- Could I do with having a little more investment in other areas? (The answer for most of us is *yes*)
- Where could I start? What could I *do* to adjust it? What could I do to start making change *today*?

***

I've had a lot of fun with this tool.

One professional athlete dealing with the end of a sporting career – and the shame that had accompanied his exit – listened intently as we segmented his pizza. He understood he had some work to do in reshaping his identity away from sports.

But then, with a gleam in his eye, he said: 'I have one problem with your model.'

I waited.

'I'm a KFC man. Have you got anything for that?'

The Greatest Love of All (or Not)

When I first heard about self-love in my teens, I was blown away by the idea that you could – and even should – like yourself *more* than anyone else. I mean, really? I had no idea about how to go about this but in theory it sounded like a free pass to Disneyland, particularly when you were still in line for your first kiss.

Since then, the concept of loving yourself has been thrashed to self-help death: 'If you don't love yourself you can't possibly love others, the first person you need to fall in love with is yourself, you need to be your own BFF' and all those other clichés that make our eyes glaze over. People are even marrying themselves now, which I understand on some level because it can promote healing from a toxic partner or traumatic relationship history. Still, it's a lot of expense when you could get the same effect from slipping on a great outfit, lighting a candle and pouring yourself a very large drink.

Self-love is a little like marriage in this, though. You wouldn't marry someone you didn't know well – or at least you shouldn't. You'd invest time in getting to know them, their hopes and dreams, how they think and feel, how they react and roll in the world. But when it comes to ourselves we are sloppy; we don't give our primary relationship the time and attention it needs. We don't get to know ourselves, which makes no sense at all when this relationship is a done deal.

Besides, I always say to people, you're stuck with yourself. Wouldn't it be great if you liked each other?

***

'What do you think of yourself?' I ask everyone I meet. Okay, not people I meet socially or in the street; that would be a fairly lonely path to take.

But I do ask clients to glean valuable information about how they see, relate and function in the world. Even the way someone looks at you when you ask the question can tell you something interesting. I've been met with a lot of nervous laughter and an equal amount of silence; I've had people who couldn't look at me, such was the level of their shame or shyness, and one young man whose body tremors shook him from one end of the couch to the other and back again before he said a word. One woman burst into tears and ran from the room. No prizes for guessing where her self-worth rating sat; no prizes for guessing who had to run down the hall after her, and in doing so address her own insensitivity rating.

You must take care asking about self-worth because for many people it is not just a question. It can tap something deep, pain they've carried for a long time. It can tear open a wound they tried to fool themselves was healed even though they knew it wasn't. So you need to respect all that goes with such a question, something I learned as I pursued that distressed woman. She did come back, to my relief, and she was wonderful.

As a concept, self-worth (also known as self-esteem) has its critics because it's both hard to measure and a moving target. It can and does fluctuate between ages, stages and circumstances, as well as between the different compartments of our lives. For example, a woman who feels great about herself in the corporate arena may be highly vulnerable in her intimate relationships because she has never had a long-term relationship. Or a man who knows his worth as a husband and dad may hate his body because he has a binge-eating problem and his weight keeps ticking up. But because the way we feel about ourselves has such an influence on our lives, it's helpful to explore it – and to find ways to boost it.

How to Like Yourself Without Feeling Stupid

When you think about it, your relationship with yourself is the most fundamental of your life. So it makes sense to try to make it as good as possible. It's especially important when being Busy as F*ck rocks our world: a solid self-foundation helps immensely.

Even people who struggle to like themselves want to know how – for their kids. I've never seen a parent who didn't want, at least in theory, their kids to prosper, mentally, physically (and financially helps too). 'I don't want him/her to feel about herself the way I always have,' they'll say, and that's a worthy goal.

But they're extremely wary of calls to stand in front of the mirror chanting affirmations on how fabulous they are. Or channelling their inner rock star (who does that and how?) or writing soppy love notes to themselves.

I don't blame them; I wouldn't do that either. Gimmicks won't work because they're not founded on anything real. The trick is to base your efforts on evidence for the person you really are and the things you really do.

So try these strategies: you have to lock them in and practice, though; one-off attempts won't go the distance.

Identify What Is TRUE

Pick one of your good qualities (more detail on strengths in the confidence booster below). Hopefully, you have a lot to choose from – but one is a good start. For example, if you are a kind person, just remind yourself you are kind, run through a couple of recent (within the past week) signs of your kindness, then go do something kind. After that, move onto another strength and repeat. Keep a record of these – it's a really good pick-me-up when you're not feeling great.

PRAISE What You've DONE

When we're not in a good space we often dismiss our genuine efforts, and the good things we've done, as not good enough. Or we look back on our lives and think we haven't done much (or enough) with them – when we have. All lives contain triumphs and feel-good moments. It's really helpful to record things you've done in the past – it balances things out when you are feeling low.

Notice your *achievements*, however small, and give yourself a tick. So if you want to lose weight and you've been for a brisk walk, praise yourself for that specific act, tell yourself you took a positive step towards your goal. Do a fist pump – say *yeeesss*!

THINK Before You ASK

When faced with a problem or dilemma, pause – give yourself time to think it through before rushing to ask for help or giving up. Slow down and try. You'll be surprised how often you find a solution. This promotes self-efficacy, an 'I can do things' belief.

Hang Out ALONE

Some people struggle to spend time alone contentedly; they rely on drawing energy from others and/or they can't face exposure to their own insecurity. It's also a trap to position and define yourself against others: people, even friends, can be fickle, and when you are forced to be alone you'll feel anxious. Take yourself on a date to somewhere you've never been – it'll feed your creativity.

Give Yourself a Daily COMPLIMENT

Don't overdo it or you'll feel weird. Just pick on one thing you're genuinely pleased with, and don't make it all about your physical appearance.

Use Your BODY (Not Just for Flaunting, Adorning or Sex)

Move, be physical, walk, take the stairs, stretch. It need not be a strenuous workout but go ahead if you'd like to. Using your body helps connect mind and body (a disconnection between mind and body can be a significant problem – see Your Body is Not a Temple, p. 254).

FINISH Things

Not every little thing, always. But persistence is a good quality and completion (of anything, no matter how small) equals achievement. Recording your achievements is great too (see *Praise What You've Done*, previous page).

Cut Talking CRAP About Yourself

Positive self-talk is useless – unless you fully believe it. So start by knocking the negatives about yourself on the head. Every time you start beating up on yourself or hear that inner critic whisper – say *no*. Replace it with 'I'm okay' instead.

Keep Personal HYGIENE Standards High

I don't need to explain this one. Hopefully.

Be a FRIEND

Be a friend, not a sucker nor a rescue pup, but a reliable friend. To people you don't know, be friendly. Be polite – it's the easiest way to get good feedback from the world. And don't be (purposefully) mean: you'll never feel good about yourself if you are mean.

Don't COMPARE

Comparison is the thief of self-worth, as well as a great promoter of anxiety – and social media doesn't help. The online world makes it seem as though everyone is doing greater, cooler, more fun things than you (even though they're not). When you find yourself comparing yourself to anyone, or their achievements, stop and distract! Go immerse yourself in something of your own.

Say What You ENJOY

If you enjoy something, tell people. It helps validate your own interests; it builds your confidence in doing them. Saying yes to what you enjoy is often an easier strategy than saying no to things.

CLEAN UP

Your space, your room, any messy relationships, your life. I'm not your mother and I don't want to sound like her, but do it. Enticing environments – or having one space you like to be in – promote healthy internal feelings.

A Quick Confidence Booster

One of the key pieces of work psychologists do is help people work out their anchors – what really matters to them – and how to stay aligned with them.

Sometimes we'll access this through their values but when asked about these things we tend to be unoriginal, rolling with the same things as everyone else: honesty, integrity, trust, compassion … yawn. That's fine in theory but we don't always stick to them and those things don't give us a point of difference.

It's more powerful – and more relevant – to tap instead into strengths. There we find the keys to our true nature and the ways we are best suited to make our unique contribution to the world. You can add skills, and you can shore up your weaknesses, but your strengths reveal who you truly are.

So try this three-step exercise:

1. Write down your top three strengths. Not work-related either; make them about who you are as a person. (Note: do this by yourself, without leaning on a strengths finder tool.)

Many people find this tough because they get caught up in what they're not good at – and haven't given any thought to their own skills.

2. When you've got your list, come up with a recent piece of evidence for each. What behaviour did you do in the past week

to prove it? For example, if you said you were creative, what have you done in those seven days to demonstrate it?

You'll begin to embed self-knowledge and belief in the things you are good at. You'll also begin to notice your strengths when you use them – and bring them into every area of your life.

> Example: If you said you were creative, don't confine it to that thing you do when no-one is watching. You should use it daily – in your chores, activities, conversations, where you go, who you talk to. You should find an avenue for demonstrating your creativity at work, no matter how small. If this is not possible, pay attention: it might not be the role for you.

For Your Kids (and You)

It's hugely important to teach your children to identify and use their strengths, but don't let yourself off the hook. Tapping your strengths will help you build resilience for when the winds of change, or the Perfect Storm, rolls in.

Keep a record of your strengths – in your phone is ideal. Simply looking at the list is a good pick-me-up when you're feeling down.

Anahera's Story

Self-esteem remained a theoretical concept to me until, as a newly minted psychologist, I met Anahera, a sweet and disarmingly open 14-year-old Māori girl who'd been sent along for a psychological assessment.

She'd been through a string of foster homes while her mother was in drug addiction treatment. She didn't know who her father was and her three siblings, to other fathers, were scattered around the district.

Anahera told me she was being pressured for sex by an older boy in her latest foster home – she didn't want to have sex with him but she probably would.

'Why?' I asked. Some of my questions were horribly naive back then.

'I have a low self-esteem.'

Sometimes the most telling information is delivered to you not in the words themselves but the way they are said. Anahera used the term 'self-esteem' like you would a body part, a heart or lungs, something you were born with, something that was just wired in. She didn't know what it meant, only that hers was low and that meant you did whatever anyone told you to do. The boy in the foster home had given her that label (naturally, he told her he had a high self-esteem) and was using it to manipulate her.

'Self-esteem is not something you are born with,' I said to Anahera, struggling to explain. 'It's about thinking good things about yourself and you can learn ways to do that.' But the words sounded hollow, even to me, because while she may not have been born with her beliefs, her life circumstances had set her up for them.

Unsurprisingly, she struggled to grasp my clumsy explanation. The boy in the foster home had done his work well and I couldn't help but think he'd used that line successfully before.

Anahera was removed from the home after her disclosure, and her therapy sessions terminated, but I have never forgotten her wide smile and her steady belief in her own lack of worth – a label forced on her in childhood – and where it was likely to land her.

Many times, I have wondered how her life panned out. One of the most difficult parts of this job is getting to know the beginning of someone's story, sometimes in raw, intimate detail, and learning to live with not knowing the ending.

And, even if you did, that it would not be at all what you hoped for.

What Do You Want?

Frankie is on a mission to save the world – but she's utterly miserable.

A straight-A student at school, she has long dreamed of working as a doctor in developing countries. She'd studied almost to breaking point to get into medical school and had been so excited about the future. But now, in her second year at university, the balloon has popped. Her grades have fallen and she's feeling flat and anxious.

'I'm not even sure I still want to be a doctor,' she says, looking almost too washed out to tell her story.

Slowly, Frankie reveals her glittering history. From her early school years she'd made a smash success of everything she touched. Her studies. Dance. Debating. Piano. Head Girl at her high school. Because she'd done so well – great grades, passing scholarship and piano exams, winning competitions, being selected for leadership roles – she kept raising the bar on herself. Now, when she can't hit those dizzy heights, she feels she is failing. The only solution she can see is to ditch medicine for a different career, one she can excel at.

When I try to return her to past successes, Frankie shows little interest. She's focused on her current troubles, excessively beating up on herself for mistakes, especially her falling grades, which are still excellent. She is fearful about trying anything new – she can't remember the last time she tried. 'If I can't be the best, why bother,' has become her mantra.

Frankie is exhibiting the two key characteristics of a perfectionist personality style – in spades.

1. Setting unreasonably high standards for yourself and others (and becoming disappointed or critical when these standards aren't met). It can fuel a pervasive fear that you are not good enough – and never will be.
2. Zeroing in on flaws and mistakes in your own accomplishments at the expense of all the great things you do or have done.

Like all perfectionists, Frankie uses an 'all or nothing' framework so she thinks in extremes: good or bad, brilliant or terrible, success or failure. It can paralyse decision-making or stepping into the unknown; anything in the middle can make them anxious. Perfectionists are also driven by thoughts of 'I should' or 'I must', which means they constantly try to do the right thing at the expense of spontaneity, creativity – and fun.

A psychologist shouldn't tell an ambitious young person to 'lower' their standards or not go all out in pursuit of their dreams. That would be unfair, potentially even damaging. They'll wonder *which* standards to drop, which increases anxiety.

But you can help them think less about what they want from life and more about the life they want.

So I ask, 'What's fun for you, Frankie?'

She stares at me blankly, so I try again. 'What do you do for fun? For no purpose other than it makes you feel good?'

'I don't know,' she finally says. 'Hanging out with my friends, I suppose. Instagram seems like a pathetic answer. I've got so much I have to do all the time. Nothing feels fun anymore.'

Frankie's case is common – young people who've been star performers in school can struggle when their achievements level out. One of the smartest girls at her high school, she is middle-of-the-pack at medical school, and this comes as a blow to her – especially when she realises hard work (her secret weapon) isn't enough to topple the competition.

Adding to Frankie's difficulties was that her life had always been heavily scheduled, first by her parents, then her school roles and activities; she had always just had to turn up, put her head down, get on with it – and success would happen. Now she's living in a flat with others: she has life decisions to make as well as study ones, admin and chores to do and a whole lot of things that are new to her. It is the first time her intelligence, as she sees it, has let her down. The stress feels overwhelming.

Perfectionist struggles are becoming widespread as we see – or can't avoid seeing – what everyone else is doing. While not everyone is a perfectionist, we can all wobble when we don't meet our own expectations. Some say depression can be measured by the gap between *where you are now* and where you *hoped you'd be* – and this can happen at any age. That's why mid-life is a common point of disillusionment: when we realise we are not where we planned to be (or with whom we'd lusted after) – and it feels too hard to change it.

We are happiest when we are striving, even though we don't always know it: passing exams, chasing university degrees or trade qualifications, getting the first job (then the next job), dropping 10 kg, lifting bigger weights, running faster times, saving a house deposit, getting the white picket fence, having a child, raising a family (then setting goals for them). All of that drives us forward, gives us a reason for getting out of bed, a sense of achievement – particularly when we're good at it. In other words, when we are Busy as F*ck achieving, it is (sort of) okay. But when we lose our structure, reach a fork in the road or fall short of our dreams and plans, angst creeps in.

While it's fantastic to aim high and fulfil our capabilities, we all stutter, stumble and stall – and if we don't allow for this, we're putting our mental health and happiness at risk. So while these tips are for Frankie, and others like her, we can all use them to shift to a healthier approach.

How to Do Things (a Little) Badly

* Shrink Your Mistakes

When you make a mistake, don't allow it to take over. Allow yourself to feel the distress – but then counter it with a positive, something good you've done.

* Shrink Other People's Mistakes

Perfectionists are particularly quick to judge others – but we all can be guilty of this. Seek to understand someone's actions or behaviour and, before calling it out or making a rash judgment, wait to see if this is a pattern rather than a single mistake. Understand that we are all flawed so don't discard people too quickly.

* Keep Yourself in the Middle

Set process (or learning or dating) goals rather than outcomes or results. While it's difficult to put the outcome out of your mind altogether, focus on what you can learn or what you can enjoy. Keep goals achievable, and update them as you go.

* Do Things for Fun (Rather than Pure Achievement)

Perfectionists can't help but look for that tick on their CV, that A+ grade or that trophy partner. Heavy focus on outcome can make you fear failure or scared to try. Focus instead on lightening up and having a good time.

* Drop the Mask, at Least with Your Friends

Having excessively high standards can make you hard work as a friend as you always act as though all is well (and successful) in your world. It's okay to talk about your mistakes and confess when you are struggling; it makes you more human and more real.

* Try Something New Every Week

Spontaneity is important – and attractive. Experiment and try new things (even if you have no skill or aptitude for them) to break your 'should' and/or 'must' style of operating.

* Do Things Badly Sometimes. Please.

It'll (sort of) set you free.

***

Wands, Miracles and the Strange Quest for Happiness

'What do you want?' I'll ask people, when they're ready. I'm talking about what they want from our sessions, of course, but I'm also leaving it open in case they want to take it bigger, to offer up their goals for life.

In Frankie's case, we had to peel things back. With her Busy as F*ck life revolving entirely around her medical studies, she felt like she was failing as a person. She didn't need any more talk about what she wanted from life; she needed to reset, to engage with other interests so she viewed herself as a young woman, rather than a would-be (and failing) doctor. Her study slice of pizza had gotten way too big.

But I love asking people, 'What do you want?' – it's super-important.

A few find it easy to answer. Others stutter and stammer: often they have thought so long and hard about what they don't want, that's what their thoughts are snagged on.

'I don't want to feel this way,' they'll say, so I'll press a little harder.

'What do you mean by this way?'

'Stuck.'

And they'll return to symptoms – the prickling anxiety, the flat mood, the dread, the things that make them uneasy about getting out of bed and facing life every day. Or the burden of all they have to do. Or the uncertainty, and fear, about what lies ahead.

'But those are all the things you don't want,' I'll say. 'Tell me what you do want. Tell me how you'd like things to be.'

Then, if that's too hard, I use the miracle question, the one we're taught to ask as interns, the one that always makes me feel like I should have a wand in my hand. (I have got a wand, by the way; it's purple plastic with a star on the end. I interned at a service for troubled kids and our inspired supervisor gave us all wands and insisted we carry them in our diaries. Although I was too shy to ever wave it, it did make me feel more powerful. I keep the wand in a drawer these days.)

'If you could change anything about your life in the next year, what would it be?'

It may surprise you, but many people have not truly thought about they want, not in preparation for our session or our work, but from life. It strikes me as odd you would put more effort into planning a weekend away than you would into your life. But it's also exciting because just identifying how someone would like things to be can make a huge difference – quickly.

'We need to work out what matters to you because we can't hit a target we can't see.'

I'm conscious not all psychologists do this and goal setting may be the fallout of all my years playing sports, but I like to know what we are working towards. I don't want to just alleviate distressing symptoms, to stop tears, turn off anger or stymie panic. I want to know what *means something* to someone, not just what makes them tick – but what makes them hum. I want a higher goal. I want it for me, I confess. But, even more, I want it for everyone I work with. I want people to have a reason for showing up, not to therapy, but for themselves – and for their lives.

I want us all to have a *why*.

***

'I just want to be happy,' people say.

I wait. We *all* want to be happy. That's why, like weight loss, happiness has burgeoned into an industry. There are blogs, books, online courses, webinars and retreats. The people who write and run these are very smart, and getting very rich, because they know everyone is chasing something that can't be caught.

Of the hundreds, maybe thousands, of people I've asked what they want from life, by far the most common answer has been happiness. But, when pressed, most find it hard to articulate what happiness is or looks like, maybe because they've never tried to unpack it, to work out what it might mean to them.

Ask any parent what they want for their kids and they can't lay their lips around the cliché quickly enough. I just want (insert child's name here) to be happy. They make a fair point too; by the time you've been through the trials of raising teenagers you care less about their career prospects and how much money they're making: a little bit of happiness will do nicely, thanks.

So it's fair to want happiness for our kids – and less angst for ourselves.

But we need to stop there.

Because telling young people we want them to be happy is the tallest order of all. I mean, how many people do you know who are swimming in joy juice? I haven't met many and when I do I remember them.

One of the worrying trends in society is the number of young people who are struggling at a time in their lives when they should be excited about the future. Instead, they are frozen by choice, indecisive and anxious about racking up debt: What should I study? What career path should I take? What if I make the wrong choice? What if I waste time and money? What if I let people down? What if I don't live up to the dream (mine and everyone else's)? What if others get ahead of me?

They're also fearful about the state of the world. It's not surprising: while global connectedness has brought us closer, it's not all in a good way. A rotating news feed of strife, sadness, distress and pain carves into our psyches – especially when we are young and haven't known any other way. An uncertain world breeds fear in its occupants. What's going to happen to the planet? The environment? The people? Should I bring kids into this world? Is all this effort worth anything?

So happiness is often not something young people can comprehend, let alone chase down. Besides, their concept of a happy life and relationship can be (sadly) quite different from the one we have modelled to them.

We can't change the complex, crazy world we're living in, but we can release the pressure valve on our kids and youth by giving them better advice or, where appropriate, no advice at all.

Here are a few (well-meaning) tips to point the fresh-faced toward happi(er)ness.

You Don't Need a Grand Plan

Just start something. Part of the fun of life is *not* knowing where it's going. Clarity of purpose is a fine aim but not very realistic when you are young and living in the 21st century. Trying too hard to figure out the endgame takes away the pleasure of the moment and applies pressure you don't need – and may not yet be equipped to handle. Besides, a little uncertainty can be fun.

Don't Do What You Love. Do What Intrigues You.

Give up the passion hunt. Only a rare few have their pathway lit from a very early age. Most of us need to explore, try things, stumble and mess up. All of it adds to your knowledge, experiences and perspective. So go be curious, and learn things, instead.

A Single Decision Doesn't Matter

Decisions come and go. So do choices. Whatever choice you are facing won't be the last one you ever have so don't give it that much power. Over-hyping it will make you fearful and timid when it's better (and healthier) to go bold. Even if it doesn't work out you'll learn things.

All Paths Lead to Somewhere (or Other)

Nothing is wasted. Even that monotonous minimum-wage job you think is beneath you has something to offer or to teach you. Your mission is to look for it.

Jump in with Two Feet

Whatever you do, throw your heart over the bar. Being one foot in, one foot out prevents you from fully engaging with anything, from jobs to interests to relationships. Don't be half-hearted about your life. Deliver your whole self to the task at hand and see what happens.

Who You Are Trumps What You Do

Instead of focusing solely on your career, just aim to be a person in the world. Don't aim to be the biggest, highest, grandest version of that person either – it's way too soon for that kind of pressure.

Just dive in and live decently and well. Trust that who you are will form in time.

Keep Your Tank Topped Up
Self-care, learning, creativity and nourishment are huge. Build up tools and strategies to arm you for the crap that invariably comes to all of us. Keep your personal tank full so you can reach in when you're struggling as well as reach out to others when you need to.

It's Okay to Do Things Just for Fun
Anything counts. As long as you're not hurting yourself or anyone else. Laugh long and loud at nothing much. The world doesn't have enough joy in it.

Two Lessons in Happiness

In the early stages of working with someone psychologically, you have to be sensitive to their views of the future. In asking what they want, you have to work out where they are at – and you have to match that with what you send them out into the world to do.

Often it's just a matter of working out *what will make the most difference to a person's life right now.* It doesn't have to be epic. They don't have to perform live on stage to thousands, build a six-figure online business, win the world champs, or meet a life partner – not after one hour, anyway. They just need something that makes them feel change is underway. Small steps like this make a solid start:

- Riding an elevator alone
- Getting through an evening without drinking wine or eating chocolate
- Being able to take negative feedback from the boss

- Going for a walk around the block after work
- Doing an exam without hyperventilating
- Starting that creative project that you keep putting off
- Listening properly to your partner

I learned not to push too hard the way we, unfortunately, learn most of our best life lessons: by messing up. I was working with a woman who had severe post-traumatic stress disorder (PTSD) following years of domestic violence. She had chronic pain, which flared every day at 6 pm, the time her partner used to arrive home and, if the mood struck him, beat her – to the point of hospitalisation, several times.

We'd been talking about what makes her happy and I asked her to show me how she saw her future. That would have been okay if I'd kept it in the room and kept it specific to what she was looking forward to at the weekend. But I was fresh and eager to help her so I asked if she'd like to present it in a picture for our next session. She had an artistic background, so she bounced out the door full of enthusiasm.

She came back with a large square board, painted black. It had caused her a lot of distress during the week, seeing a black future, a future devoid of anything. I'd delivered it to her in spades.

I was just grateful she was still alive.

It was a horrible mistake. PTSD develops from the witnessing of an event that threatens life and/or safety, and can produce a debilitating cocktail of symptoms. One of the hallmark features is not being able to form a hopeful view of the future – and, in this woman's case, I'd glossed over it. Not only had I forced her to consider the bleakness of what lay ahead, I'd left her alone with it for a whole week.

I was so worried about what I'd done, I focused the rest of our work almost solely on giving her a reason to stay alive. I changed her homework to practical tasks.

Surprisingly to me, she kept coming back and by the end of our sessions she had stuck some coloured words on her black board: TRUST. HAPPY. BALANCED. LOVE. CONTROL. NEW. SCHNUGGLING. There was a small picture of a heart and at the top a soaring bird. I still have that board. It's a reminder to me of what not to do, perhaps. But also that even someone who feels nothing for themselves or their future can begin to see possibility.

Even so, when we said goodbye, I didn't know if it would stick.

Ten years later I saw her in a gardening megastore. She looked well and happy. She had barely aged and her story reared up in my mind. She rushed over and hugged me. 'Life is wonderful,' she said, filling me in, and I could feel myself breathe out in relief.

The Happiest Woman in the World

My favourite lesson in happiness came to me from Barbara, a woman who had not wanted to meet me.

She was first person I met who did not want to change her life. Interestingly, there have not been many since. Most people want at least one thing to be different, which makes Barbara's lesson all the more memorable.

'I'm happy enough with my lot,' she said, nestling into the couch and pulling a cushion onto her knee. 'So I don't know what you're going to do about that.'

I didn't either. I'd gone into a private practice believing people would be highly motivated for change, wanting at least one aspect of their lives to be different. Up until that point, I'd seen people grappling with burnt-out or difficult relationships, their weight, money, jobs, feeling stuck, lost, passionless, desperate to find a way forward.

Not Barbara. She was in her 50s, single, with chronic type 2 diabetes and related ailments. She had been referred by her GP because she urgently needed to lose weight and be more proactive in managing her condition. My brief was to get her mind to support what her body needed.

Barbara religiously attended her sessions, was always 20 minutes early, clutching her completed homework, bright and eager to talk. She knew her physical health was declining. She had seen a photo of herself at a wedding and had mistaken herself for an elderly overweight cousin. 'I was a bit shocked at that,' she said.

But it wasn't enough to spark a change. I was frustrated: as a disciple of mind-body health, I couldn't understand anyone ignoring their physical condition when it was severely compromising her wellbeing, maybe even her life.

I encouraged her to walk more. She already did that twice daily between the bus she caught to work and her apartment, about five minutes. I pushed for tiny dietary changes. She agreed it was a good idea but she did enjoy a meat-lovers pizza of an evening. I suggested other physical activities but charity work, classic movies, making doll's house furniture and trawling second-hand shops for her china collections ate all her spare time.

Finally, I decided to put aside my ego and my goals for her and focus on hers: to keep things as they were. 'So what's so good about your life, Barbara?' I said. 'Maybe we can share your ideas with people who are less happy than you.'

She jackpot-beamed at me and rolled out a happiness checklist I couldn't fault – her tips stacked up with research, science and everything I'd ever read. More than a decade later, they still do.

Here they are:

Barbara's Top Tips for a Happy Life

Good Friends

Human connection is a time-tested contributor to our happiness and longevity. Having people who genuinely care about you matters but so does the small stuff – saying hi to retail staff, the daily smile you give to the postie, chatting to the neighbours; it all counts.

Being Helpful

Contributing to the lives of others, giving more to life than you take without exhausting yourself in the process, boosts wellbeing.

Making Things

Tapping into your creativity has multiple mental health benefits, such as the satisfaction of bringing your work into the world, distraction from problems, getting out of your head, staying in the moment. So go make stuff!

Bright Spots

Having things to look forward to (daily, weekly, monthly and long-term) elevates mood. Anticipating them puts you in a good headspace.

Time for Me

Having time to slow down, having some control over your time, helps you feel like you're running your own race. And it's healthy to have at least one way of relaxing (bringing the heart rate down) that does not involve intense activity or exercise.

Interesting Work

Feeling a sense of achievement or meaning through your work or volunteer activities makes life feel worthwhile – and that you're using time well.

Feeling Okay About Everything

I haven't seen this one on any happiness checklists. But being content with yourself and your life (in whatever form they take) may be the biggest factor of all.

* * *

'I've just loved therapy,' Barbara said at the end of her package of six sessions, rating both me and the value of the work 10/10 on a satisfaction checklist.

'Do you feel better?' I asked, a loaded question because I knew the answer.

She grinned at me as she clambered off the couch. 'No I feel the same. My life hasn't changed because I didn't want it to.' And with that she was gone, back to her evening pizza, classic movie reruns and model making.

A couple of years later I saw her boarding a city bus; her weight hadn't reduced and it was difficult for her to climb on board. But Barbara remains one of the few genuinely content people I've ever met, which caused me to rethink my views on happiness – and even mental health. *Maybe liking your life is better for your health than changing it.*

– SESSION 4 –

What's Holding You Back?

Judith is 83 when she comes to her first therapy session. She's no longer busy, she says, and that's the problem.

Judith is the oldest person I've seen by nearly 20 years, so our meeting is as much new ground for me as it is for her. But I welcome it – our burgeoning ageing population faces so many psychological and lifestyle issues: grief, loneliness, adjusting to change and losing their place and sense of value in the world. Therapy can be foreign, and even scary, territory for an older person but as long as they are up for talking to a (qualified) stranger, it can help.

Judith is struggling with lingering grief. A year earlier she'd lost her adored second husband to a stroke and hadn't been able to shake the 'black cloud' that came with her loss. She stopped going to gardening and mahjong, and began to avoid her friends when they called. Her daughter, who had booked the appointment, was worried she was shutting down her life when still in good physical health and a sociable person.

'I'm just so sad,' Judith says, at her first session. 'Charlie was the love of my life. I waited so long to find him.'

Judith comes to each session immaculately dressed, always with a neat string of pearls for the occasion. She is mentally sharp and more open than you might expect a woman of her age to be.

Her stories are detailed and colourful, depicting a life that had often been difficult, until she met Charlie.

'My first husband was a bully. He provided well for the family, so we had a good life in that way, but he wasn't someone you could warm to. He never hit me but he could say cruel things.'

'Did you ever think of leaving?'

'Oh, I never would have left him. Where would I have gone? What would I have done for money? And we had four children ... my life was really all about them. It was very difficult at times, but I kept my counsel. We had some good times too. I focused all my time and energy on the children. Is it too awful to say I secretly jumped for joy when he died?'

The Timeline

Judith agrees to do a timeline of the events in her life. I always use timelines; they're a useful way to take someone's history without getting lost in it.

It works like this: draw a line from birth to the age you are now, showing the ups and downs of your life. Label each of these peaks and troughs. Marriage. Divorce. Death of a Parent. Onset of an illness. Birth of a child. A special trip, and so on. It brings to the surface the key events in your life, or at least those that have stood out for you. The range of things people pinpoint is vast; sometimes they are major life events, sometimes they are tiny things that they believe have influenced the course of their lives.

It can also help people to take perspective: all lives have highs and lows, even the most difficult, or most happy, of them. If you are going through a tough time, it can help to see that it hasn't always been that way: there has been much achievement, and fun and laughter too. I deliberately keep the brief for doing a timeline simple so people can put their own spin on it, and give it as much, or as little, effort as they choose. Most people love doing timelines;

some come up with elaborate charts, complete with colour codes and photographs but even those who are not so invested will take the time to scratch out a quick line drawing.

Occasionally, it's a stressful exercise for people, because it can open up old wounds. When this happens we tread carefully; we chart the events together.

Judith chuckles as she hands me a fat scroll tied up with a ribbon. It stretches out the door of my office and right across the waiting room. 'It was like writing a book. A lot of things happen in 83 years.'

Judith is intrigued by therapy – 'what a great invention for people' – finding it useful to recall and capture her life. She talks about raising her children, her first husband's drinking and affairs, his erratic moods and emotional control, the stoic face she presented to the world (and even her friends) as his wife. 'No-one ever knew the real me,' she says. 'And I put in a lot of effort to keep it that way.' She spoke of finding true love at the age of 75: 'I'm so lucky I found Charlie ... it just ended all too soon.'

Judith enjoys revisiting her life. But after three sessions she says she'd like to do something else: she'd like to work more on herself. Long buried under the labels of obedient fifth child in a family of eight, controlled wife and loving mother, she'd never had a full sense of who she was. She wanted to know more.

I loved that. I loved that you could be into your 80s and still want to make your life better, that you would still think you were worth investing in.

Because it's true.

It is never too late to shake off the shackles of a troubled past, challenge a negative label or let go the critical feedback you've had from the world. It's important to remember no matter who you are, or where you stand, there is always a way forward. There is always a way to find meaning.

***

One of the key pieces of work psychologists do is to unpack the stories that define us (make up of our beliefs, labels, thoughts, feelings and behaviour) because they are barriers to change.

Judith had lost not only her partner and the life they were forging together, but her feeling of worth as a person and a member of society – and that was driving a grief which had morphed into a state of mild depression. Older people are particularly vulnerable to depression as they struggle to find purpose beyond their working years. In other words, not being Busy as F*ck can be the biggest challenge of all.

Judith had always been, as she said, of the 'stiff upper lip' brigade: keep your emotions under control; never fully reveal what you are thinking. With Charlie she had lowered her guard – 'He was the only person who really knew me, and that includes my children.' Now, she needed help to reconfigure her final years. But the process is the same as any person looking to make a change: identify what is keeping us stuck or what may block the way forward. And the roots of these can often be tracked to our past.

We Talk About the Past (a Bit)

My first career was in journalism. At one point, I worked as a magazine feature writer. I was asked to write about primal scream therapy, the baby of psychotherapist Arthur Janov, which argues neurosis is caused by repressed childhood trauma. It meant I had to lie on a yoga mat in a dim room, waiting for old pain to surface and then, I suppose, scream myself free. When nothing came out, not even a whisper, a bearded man named Richard gently told me I wasn't right for this work because I wasn't ready to deal with my past.

Perhaps I was too young, or buttoned up, or there was no significant trauma in my past to bring forth, but I walked away feeling a failure and a card-carrying cynic for alternative psychotherapies. I hope I'm more open to other methods now, but I remain edgy about forcing people to dig up their own histories, believing that not everyone carries old wounds and, even if they do, they may not need (or want) to scream about them.

Some do, though, and it is a fundamental part of the psychologist's job to work out the difference.

***

Psychology has a reputation for wallowing in the past that probably kicked off with Freud. Beyond the links to sex and fraught relationships with our mothers, he left us with a legacy we've never been able to shake: that therapy involves lying on a couch trawling our history with a silent note-taking stranger.

A teenaged boy who'd been sent along by his mother once told me he was so relieved when the hour was up because he thought he'd have to lie there, pouring out his feelings from childhood.

'Well, that's what you did, isn't it? Without the lying down part?'

'Yes, I did. I couldn't shut myself up.'

Psychologists do have couches – me included – but people mostly sit on them and that's about where the creepiness ends. You don't have to dig into the inner reaches of your inner anything – you are free to say as much or as little as you want, although being as honest as you can will give you a better deal. And if the person you are talking to is skilled they will guide you, but not take you down a series of rabbit holes.

Psychologists are supposed to ask only questions that inform the situation, or for the greater good of the person in the room. You can't trawl for information just because it interests you. A young woman who was running a second job as an assistant dominatrix once wanted to give me a full brief on her role, which she described as the same as mine but with different tools ('We're both being paid for giving people what they need'). As intrigued as I was – as much as these are the war stories you want to gather for your personal knowledge and the novel you will never write – it is not acceptable to go there. She was disappointed and, if I'm honest, so was I.

You don't *have* to go into your past. Any therapist who drags you there is not just unprofessional, they're a bit mean. But if you want to get the most from the work, there is benefit in lifting the lid on your history because it fills out the story. You are not who you are today because you landed here in a spaceship; you are the sum total of all that went before and all you believe to be true. But we need to only dig up enough of the past to understand the present. We don't need to set up camp back there, blaming your mother's mood swings or your father's total disinterest in you or crazy great-aunt Martha who was 'taken away' in the dead of night never to be seen again (everybody worries they have a crazy great-aunt Martha who will reincarnate herself in them, by the way). Dwelling on those things won't change your life. It will help you understand your past, but it won't free you from it. And the more important thing is the person you are now, the life you have now – and the life you want to live.

Some therapy models focus on the past; the work takes months or even years. Others ignore the past and claim they can change lives in a single session. And although I wouldn't advocate for this, it can happen. I've seen it. I've seen a 60-year-old man break down sobbing when he realised he wasn't a prisoner to the quiet, careful life he'd been living because he'd been diagnosed with depression 30 years earlier. I've seen his stoic wife cry quietly because she'd been living that life with him. I saw the light in their eyes when it occurred to them everything had changed in that moment, then the terror because they had no idea how to absorb that change. *What will the next 20 years look like? Will we know how to be together without depression?*

Those of us who work in brief therapy have different beliefs too. My training is in cognitive behavioural therapy (CBT), which favours a brief approach (3–12 sessions) to modify unhelpful thoughts, emotions and behaviour. It focuses on what's happening right now. But I don't stick slavishly to a CBT model because I can do more for people if I draw bits and pieces from other theories to make them a model all of their own.

While you need to deal up-front with any symptoms (like locking in coping strategies for panic attacks), to fully understand the situation you need a sense of where a person has come from, and the meaning they draw from their history and experiences.

So I say something like this: 'We can't change the past but we need to know something about it in order to change the present. What do you think?'

A few will firmly draw the rug over it: *I'm not going there. I've done the past to death with another therapist. I only want to talk about the present.*

You have to respect that; it's their choice.

A few will firmly draw the rug over it, then tell you everything. Then suddenly realise what they've done. *Oh no. Didn't mean to go there. Again.*

But most people sigh with relief. While they agree the past is part of their story, they don't want to drown in it; they'll dip their toe in but they want to stay out of the swamp.

That's all the leave pass I need: accepting that bad or difficult things have happened – not that these things were okay – is part of the healing process.

Because I offer brief therapy, people enter our work knowing they have a finite number of sessions. They can extend if necessary, or return later on, but at the outset they know it is a brief package. I like working this way because it puts a fence around what we are doing and it puts the pressure on us both to get something done. We can't get complacent; we both focus and do our homework, which gives us the best chance of success. Working in small chunks can also be easier to absorb.

Call me biased but I think brief therapy suits a Busy as F*ck world; people have constraints around time and money. As much as the idea of years of self-examination appeals to some, the world is all about immediate gratification. *When we want it, we want it now.* Sometimes, I wish it wasn't, but you have to meet the market.

It doesn't mean you never see each other again either. Once a relationship is established, it's easy to go back. Many clients I've known for a long time will return years after our original meeting just for an hour or two to chew over a specific problem.

That's rewarding because you get an update on the person's story. It's like catching up with old friends: between visits people have gone through university, married, divorced, bought and sold houses, had babies, moved overseas, had kids leaving home, loved ones pass on – and a myriad of events in between. People live and die and struggle and flourish. Life is sometimes gut-wrenchingly hard, sometimes crazily wonderful, but always, always, it chugs forward. It is hard to be part of someone's life so briefly, and so intensely, then just erase it from your mind.

You don't forget.

People will come up to you years later at a movie or on the street and say, 'Remember me?' The subtext is: 'Of course you remember me; I've told you things I've never told anyone else.' This can catch you out because, in this moment, people are not aware of how much time has elapsed or how much they've changed. Women in particular, with new haircuts and colours, and different styles, are frequently unrecognisable. But if they drop a clue, I can almost always remember their story. Sometimes it's random things like the names of the partner they weren't having sex with, or that their mother kept six bottles of gin in her garage, or that they used to dream of dead bodies, or that they went to Korea for a nose job, or that their child refused to eat fruit. My head is filled up with those stories.

Others see and avoid me. I've see them glance my way in the supermarket then take a sharp turn into the pasta aisle, when they never wanted pasta. I don't blame them. I know too much.

What Makes a Person in the World

While we each have a unique footprint, the key influences are the same for everyone. Our biology (genetics), the environments we grow up in and our life experiences all come together to form us. They lead us to develop core or deep beliefs that underpin who we are and affect our thoughts, emotions and behaviours. The feedback we get from the world further sculpts our view of ourselves. If our core beliefs are negative, we are more likely to focus on the unhelpful messages that support them. And that's what keeps us stuck.

Although psychology's reputation rests largely on what's going on in the head, it's more than that: our thoughts, emotions and behaviours combine to give us a unique operating system that governs how we roll in the world – that's what psychologists help people figure out.

In terms of what's going on in our minds, there are four key areas:

- Labels – often given to us in childhood and which we continue to conform to.
- Thoughts, which are sometimes distorted.
- Emotions, which can be poorly expressed – or locked up altogether.
- Beliefs, strongly held and often false, which have become ingrained.

Let's take a look at each.

Ouch! Labels that Hurt

Like any psychologist, I've seen the impact of negative labels picked up in childhood, at home, at school or from the mean boys (or girls) in the back of the school bus. Tags like *I'm stupid. I'm fat. I'm ugly. I can't do maths. I'll never get a girl/boy friend. I'm bad at sports* have a nasty habit of sticking around and it becomes a big job to shift them.

And yet, labels that might seem enviable can hurt too. I saw a young woman after she'd had a depressive breakdown. She'd been an exceptional contemporary dancer, her sister an equally talented swimmer – so good that they'd each won scholarships to American universities. From a very early age, they became known at home, school, and even by their parents' friends, as 'the dancer' and 'the swimmer'. They spent all their time training, competing and socialising within those worlds. Their labels became who they were. When this young woman broke down from the stress of competitive dance and had to quit, she didn't just lose her label, she lost herself. *Who am I without dancing? Who was I ever? Who likes me as a person?* She had to begin again but with time and effort she grew a great deal from the experience.

Another young woman was labelled 'the pretty one' in her family of four girls. As a child, she was the one rolled out at parties by her proud parents because she was so cute – her sisters, by contrast, were 'the brainy one', 'the sporty one' and 'the musical one'. Such was the focus on her attractiveness, her face, body and presentation, it became all-consuming for her. By her mid-teens, she had developed an eating disorder and learned to get her way with promiscuous sexual behaviour. Even though she was bright, she dropped out of university because she had no belief in her intellect. In her 40s, when I met her, she still struggled with her eating and weight, she was panicking about her retreating beauty and she could not sustain a relationship because she needed attention from multiple men – not necessarily one at a time. While she understood herself to an extent – *I'm a serial cheat. Sex is my way of being loved* – she could not figure out how to change it and that was the focus of our work.

When Thoughts Distort

Human thinking is complex: we have an estimated 50,000–70,000 thoughts per day; that's around 35–48 thoughts per minute per person. When our thinking is healthy, it can take us to the highest levels of learning and creation, but when it distorts it can leave us staggering under the impact, triggering or maintaining all manner of distress.

We all know the pain of unhealthy thinking: who hasn't lain awake at night, picking over the events of the day – of *that* conversation or *that* text message (or that lack of reply) – or what she *really* meant when she said that? Who hasn't turned the most innocuous of thoughts into a catastrophic event with disastrous consequences (that was never really likely to happen *and* never did)? Who hasn't, at some point, used whatever is trekking through their mind to beat themselves up?

So much of what goes on in our heads dictates the course of our lives. And when our lives are Busy as F*ck our thinking can be thrown into chaos, causing us to revert to old, unhelpful patterns which can shut down the ability to function. This is at odds with what we really need to do when stressed: identify our highest need, make a plan and follow it.

Everyone struggles with distorted or faulty thinking now and then. CBT proffers a series of thinking errors people make when they are struggling. See if you can identify your own patterns.

Thinking Errors

* **All or nothing – seeing things as one way or the other. No middle ground.**
  'I'm fabulous' or 'I'm useless'. 'She's hot' versus 'she is ugly'.
  'I agree with you 100 per cent' versus 'you are totally wrong.'

* **Catastrophising – believing the worst will happen based on one incident/event.**
  'I failed this paper so my law career is over.' 'I played badly
  in today's game so I will be dumped for the season.' 'She's
  working late so she must be cheating on me.'

* **Labelling – assigning a broad negative label to yourself or others.**
  'I'm stupid.' 'I'm ugly'. 'He's a bad kid.' 'He's a serial
  cheater.'

* **Filtering – zeroing in on a small (negative) aspect of an event or situation.**
  'I ate a square of chocolate today after being good all week
  so my diet is ruined.' 'I stumbled over one slide in my
  presentation today, which ruined the whole thing.'

* **Fortune-telling – predicting the future without hard evidence.**
  'She's busy at work so our relationship is going to fail.'
  'I don't like my daughter's friends because I know they'll
  lead her into drinking, drugs and sex.'

* **Personalising – taking things personally without considering other possible reasons.**
  'She didn't like my report because she hates me.' 'He
  cancelled our date because he can't stand the thought of
  being with me.'

* **Generalising – taking your interpretation of something through all aspects of your life.**
'My partner dumped me ... I'm just as useless at relationships as I am at everything else.' 'I bought a car that keeps breaking down ... I never get anything right.'

* **Blaming – focusing on someone else as the source of your negative feelings, avoiding taking any responsibility for yourself.**
'It's our coach's fault that our team lost again.' 'My parents' genes are the reason I'm fat.'

* **Mind-reading – assuming you know what people think without having sufficient evidence for their thoughts.**
'My boss thinks I'm a loser because I was late for the meeting.' 'She is saying she wants to postpone our date so she's going to dump me.'

Challenging Your Thinking

Understanding our thinking places us in a better position to come up with more rational thoughts and beliefs, and to find evidence to support those. There are many different ways to frame an event or circumstance. The person who thinks they were dumped might also have many examples showing their partner was not right for them. Or the person blaming their mother for being overweight knows they eat poorly and don't exercise. Or the person who thinks their boss hates them because they didn't comment on a paper they wrote might also rationalise their boss is Busy as F*ck – because she is. (Their boss might also be a bully but the important thing is not to lock yourself into one train of thought – particularly if you are struggling and therefore not thinking clearly about the situation).

Here are two ways to shift your thinking:

1. Find evidence. Identify your most common thinking pattern (above), isolate one of your own beliefs and come up with at least one piece of contrary evidence, as in the examples given. This takes a little practice and you may have to look for more than one piece of evidence before you are convinced. However, while this theory is sound, people sometimes still have trouble shifting their thinking.

So here is a simple goal-focused (and my preferred) way to give your thinking a nudge in a new direction.

2. Goal focus. Think about something you want. Now identify the (old) thought you are holding which is a barrier to that goal. Then come up with a (new) thought that would help you achieve it, which is a portal to getting there.

Example 1: You want a promotion at work. (Old thought: *I'm stuck in this role.*) New thought: *If I added a new skill I could make myself stand out.* The trick to embedding your new thought is to back it with action. So go and learn a new skill. That will provide evidence, to yourself as well as others, you are moving towards your goal.

Example 2: You want to write a book. (Old thought: *I'm too old/ young.*) New thought: *People of all ages write books. I'm going to start writing for myself anyway.* Action step: Write daily! And plot a string of small goals to move forward.

Example 3: You want to lose weight. (Old thought: *I always fail at diets.*) New thought: *I want to go hiking with my kids this summer.* Action step: Start a walking program. Today.

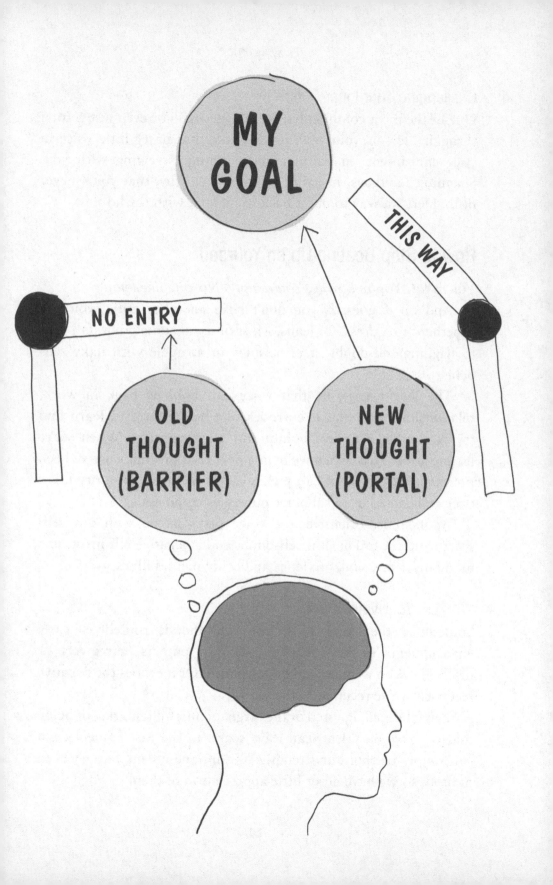

Challenging Your Inner Critic

One of the most common barriers to success – or even just getting through life – is your own inner critic, that nasty little voice in your ear, intent on baiting, undermining, screwing with you. Scanning for flaws, insisting you're not worthy, that you'll never fit in. Here's a way to put it back in its box, with the lid shut.

How to Stop Beating Up on Yourself

You're fat. You're boring. You're ugly. No-one likes you.

And on it goes. If you don't have an inner critic, you're a superhero in a dress. Or jeans. Most of us, at some point, fall prey to nagging self-doubt or criticism – or struggle with flaky self-belief.

The fear fanned by that voice can hold us back in work, relationships and life. It corrodes our best efforts to learn and try new things, to live boldly and adventurously. When we're feeling good – like when we're in a new relationship or we've been promoted at work – it can pick away at us until insecurity takes over and causes us to sabotage our own happiness.

At its most offensive, the voice plays havoc with our self-worth and mental health. Self-doubt and a negative self-image can maintain depression, anxieties and other mental illnesses.

Who Let Your Voice Out?

Sometimes the voice yaps from childhood, rooted in early environments or key people – such as parents, caregivers or teachers – who were critical or neglectful. Or it echoes the negative feedback we've received in the world.

Being bullied, ignored or the target of hurtful remarks, or being told we have no talent, can leave scars. In the case of neglect, it can simply be that our strengths and unique talents haven't been praised, so we have no or little appreciation of them.

Research indicates these people, environments or experiences take aim at a person's sense of self, either stunting its development or damaging it before it has a chance to mature. As we've discussed, you can build your self-worth, and a critical part of that is slapping a muzzle on your inner critic.

Here's how:

- **Name it.** Give your critic a name. Choose something you consider boring like, say, Kevin (apologies to any Kevins reading this but that's the name Google once identified as most unlikely to get a date). When the voice starts up with its dark chant, calmly say 'Hi, Kevin' as though you are greeting someone who doesn't interest you. It will de-power the voice.

- **Be curious.** Take an investigator's approach. What is the tone, the volume, the pitch of the voice? Is it male or female? Is it a voice you recognise? Is it always the same or does it take on different identities? Describe the voice to yourself – perhaps not out loud if you're in company. Your reputation does matter (slightly).

- **Break up with them.** You shouldn't stay in a relationship with anyone destructive or focused on holding you back, including your inner critic. When you hear the voice, remind yourself words can only sting if you attach meaning to them. You don't have to believe everything you hear. Just let the words pass by and refrain from latching onto them.

- **Replace cruel words with kinder ones.** The best way to get rid of a bad habit is to replace it with something healthier. In other words, replace your critic's nasty shots with words that make you feel good. Think of something you know to be true about yourself – it doesn't have to be related to what the voice is saying (for example, if you believe you are *kind*, then just tell yourself that you are a *kind* person.)

- **Gather evidence for the real you.** This is the most important point of all because you need to provide yourself with proof of the person you really are in the world. So if you think, or have been told, you are *kind*, go and do something – no matter how small – that reminds you of the *kind* person you really are.

That's it. Five steps. Remember, the voice is not real; it's an illusion born of your own fears. Do you really need to be afraid of yourself?

Emotions: Let Me Tell You How I Feel

Once I worked with a young woman whose response to every distressing event or interaction was to cry.

She had grown up with four older brothers who had teased her constantly and, in order to get them to let up or her parents to intervene, she would burst into tears. It worked: her parents always took her side, called the boys off (and punished them), and she got what she wanted.

Now as a third-year law student, and in her first serious relationship, the tears weren't working for her. 'I'm physically very tough – who wouldn't be when they had four big brothers – but if anything goes wrong, if I feel hurt, even the slightest thing, I'm in tears. I can cry for hours.'

When I tried to explore other possible responses, she was genuinely bewildered. 'What else could I do?' she said. She had no idea how to be with her own discomfort; she had no language for saying how she felt. And it was beginning to interfere with her work, relationship and friendships.

Our emotions are simply how we feel. *Being able to express, and regulate, our emotions is a vital cog in helping us to navigate the world successfully.* We each have our own emotional range (I call this your emotional pendulum). Some have a wide range of intense emotions; others are inexpressive, even shut down. When you understand your own pendulum (or the range and intensity of the swing) you are better placed to manage it.

YOUR EMOTIONAL PENDULUM

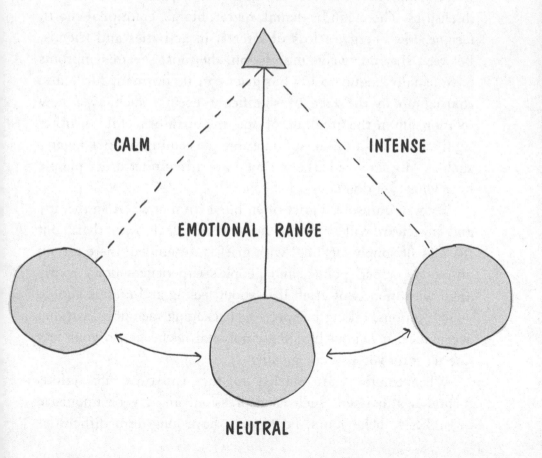

CALM

INTENSE

EMOTIONAL | RANGE

NEUTRAL

There are many reasons why people are emotionally closed or unable to manage their feelings. Loss of a loved one, a traumatic experience or a devastating change in circumstances are common pathways to emotional difficulty. Sometimes it comes from conflict or neglect in early environments or parents who did not know how to give their children sound emotional feedback: when and how to express feelings, when to pull back, when you've gone too far.

It can also occur beyond childhood, due to grief, loss or other difficult experiences. Let's examine a few of these.

Grief and Loss

Grief symptoms start off looking like depression of various intensities. There can be denial, regret, blame, emotional chaos, fatigue, low energy, a loss of interest in activities and friends. Between six and twelve months on, the most severe symptoms have usually begun to lift but grief can lie dormant for years, roaring up in the face of significant events, such as a new relationship or the break up of one, the birth of a child or other significant dates or events. Sometimes a seemingly tiny trigger – such as Mother's or Father's Day – are a reminder other people have what you don't.

Tears of unresolved grief often burst from nowhere in therapy and my client will say, 'I've never really dealt with that.' But the idea of simply 'dealing' with grief is misguided; there are no absolutes, or end points, and people's experiences don't neatly align with models of grief. It is about feeling and understanding your reactions, taking perspective, packaging memories, gaining acceptance. It's about building emotional resilience, so your loss doesn't stunt you psychologically.

When emotions are bottled up, they can turn into serious mental health issues such as depression, anxiety or impulsive or addictive behaviours. People can have long-term difficulties holding down jobs or maintaining relationships without knowing why.

There's no denying childhood loss can make it hard to love. Some people react by pushing others away because they can't bear the pain of losing love again – or even the risk. Some cling too hard to it, becoming excessively needy in their terror of loss. Others idealise the person who has gone, making it near impossible for anyone else to compete. Being able to move forward can often depend on how you view, package or let go of the one who is no longer there.

How to Show What You Feel (Appropriately)
The good – and healthy – news is that while it is ideal to start young, it is never too late to improve your emotional expression, which includes your ability to regulate your emotions, your language and behaviour.

Here are the key steps:

* Know your own reactions to distress, hurt or criticism.
It's important to be aware of your own initial response. Try this simple exercise.

When I'm stressed, my go-to reaction is:

- Cry or get angry
- Go quiet, shut down
- Get busy, distract with activity
- Go inside my head (overthink, ruminate)
- Behave in unhealthy ways (with alcohol, food, sex, drugs, cigarettes)
- Calm (think rationally and act appropriately)

There are no 'great' or 'terrible' reactions: this is about self-understanding. It is likely you do more than one of the above.

While being calm in stressful situations seems ideal, it's not if you have entrapped your feelings. It's beyond most of us to appropriately express our emotions every time, then quickly move to calm – there's at least one step in between. So choose the path you are most likely to take and ask yourself:

- What is my immediate reaction? How strong is the reaction (or how wide and vigorously does my pendulum swing?)
- How long do I spend doing this?
- Is this an appropriate amount of time? Should I boundary it?
- What else could I do to express myself?
- What could I do after that? This may be a simple activity or distraction technique to separate us from the emotions.

Remember, your go-to reaction can be changed or adjusted. And if you're okay with how you respond, it's worth keeping an eye on how long you give over to it. If it is starting to creep into other areas of your life, it may be time to put a boundary around it.

* Know it is *normal* to experience a range of emotions – and it's *okay* to feel them.

It's important to understand your emotions are not the same as your thoughts – although how you feel can be driven by the things you think about (and your thinking can obviously affect your moods). But neither emotions nor thoughts need to rule you: both can be managed or soothed.

Being able to *tolerate* intense emotions is a valuable skill. So allow yourself to *notice* and *feel* the reactions in your mind and body, and then to *sit* with them. You don't have to do anything with them.

* Learn to recognise different emotions – and be able to name them.

Many people – frequently boys and men– struggle to differentiate their feelings. When asked about how they feel, they often lump everything together under 'frustration' or 'anger'. Even sadness can be difficult to identify and express.

Having a way of speaking about emotions or feelings is a language that can be learned like any other. By labelling emotions, we learn to distinguish one from another, which both reduces the fear of being overwhelmed by feelings and enhances our ability to cope.

* Express positive emotion too.

Talk about emotions usually refers to the Bad Stuff – the things that distress us – because that's what we worry about. But in doing so we often neglect the importance of talking about the Good Stuff or, horror of all horrors, talking up ourselves. Being able to express positive emotion is equally valid. Unfortunately, there's not enough encouragement for that – it's almost like we're reluctant, even scared, to express positive feelings when so many around us are suffering. Who dares to do that? Who's *that* insensitive? We need to encourage each other to say (out loud) we feel calm and upbeat and satisfied when we do. We should be able to be proud of ourselves, and say so, without being accused of being arrogant or insensitive, especially in environments where suicide, self-harm, abuse and mental health statistics are worrying – and rising. What we talk about is contagious, particularly in tight communities or small, isolated countries, so we need to talk about good things too.

* Have at least one quick, healthy way of self-soothing.

For example, breathing techniques, quiet time, reading, music, exercise routines. But don't rush to do these before you've identified and named the feeling because you'll cut short your emotional education. You'll find breathing exercises in Session 8 (What to Do When It All Goes Wrong).

Beliefs: If You Believe It, You'll Achieve It (and That Will Keep You Stuck)

What we believe to be true dictates the course of our lives. Some of our beliefs are healthy and promote our wellbeing and success. But all too frequently, false beliefs are born in childhood and we unconsciously feed and nurture them, allowing them to rule over our thoughts, emotions and behaviour. Old beliefs need to be challenged for their truth and relevancy and in the full knowledge that they can be changed.

Think about your own beliefs about yourself for a moment. What do you hold to be true about yourself? See if you can fill in the gaps below, even if only in your head.

I am _____

I am _____

I am _____

It's likely you can think of several – hopefully some are positive. Once you understand the grip that these beliefs have on you, you can set about breaking them down.

Here are four of the most commonly reported beliefs that hold us back, along with some strategies to help:

- I'm too scared (I worry about the consequences of my actions; what if the worst happens?)
- I'm too nice (I try to keep everyone happy; I can't say no to anyone; people use me because I'm too obliging)

- I'm too sensitive (I overthink things; I'm too susceptible to criticism; I'm easily hurt)
- I'm too boring. (I don't have anything interesting to say or worthwhile to offer; no-one will ever want to be with me).

How to Stop Being Scared of Being Scared

Three Keys to Switching Your Mindset

So you're afraid? Welcome to Club Normal. We're all freaking out. Even the superficially bold, or pathologically disordered, are masking some form of insecurity. Only the degree of fear separates us.

Everyone experiences stress and worry. But when those feelings blow out of control, anxiety takes on a life of its own. We begin to worry about how we feel, why our thoughts are so dark and that we are going crazy. Nothing seems to provide any relief.

And that's scary. Because it can make us feel – wrongly – like we're broken in ways that can't be fixed.

Are You Throwing Steak at the Tiger?

Fear, boiled down, is an unpleasant emotion triggered by threat. When the threat is large enough, it can turn to terror – and sometimes there are very real reasons for that, such as when our lives or safety are in danger.

But most of the time our fears come from thoughts rather than actual threat – and *thoughts are just things*. Sometimes they are grounded in reality but far more often we fret, overthink and ruminate about 'issues' not deserving of much attention at all. Especially in the dead of night.

Fear can come in all sorts of packages; sometimes it shows up in people who, to the rest of us, look fully in control. And the discrepancy between how they look and how they feel sets up an internal conflict that can make it worse.

A young woman I saw had broken down after an extremely stressful work experience. Her friends saw her as cool and calm, the one they leaned on when they were in trouble.

'I'm desperate,' she said. 'I've been told I have all the tools inside me to fix this. But I feel horrible. How am I supposed to find anything in there – let alone the right tool?'

She had a good point. Her desperation to get rid of the feelings was keeping them alive and hungry. Desperation is anxiety's favourite snack. It's like throwing steak at a tiger.

But Wait! There Is No Tiger

Psychologists always say it's not the problem but the way we respond to it that matters. We're boring like that, but we're okay with being boring when we know it's the truth.

There are many tools and strategies for calming yourself and coping with anxiety but here's the bad news: unless they are underpinned by the right mindset, they won't keep working for you.

So before you break out the positive mantras and breathing exercises, check out these keys to priming yourself for success:

- **You are not special.** Feeling anxious can make you feel alone and conspicuous at the same time. But you're in excellent company. If we walked downtown and all the people who were feeling scared or worried had lights flashing on top of their heads, the streets would be aglow. Except in extreme cases of physiological distress, your fear is invisible. It's helpful to know you can still control how you present to the world. Even at your anxious worst, you look like any other person – as long as you are wearing clothes.
- **You don't need to tame the tiger.** Anxiety is not a wild animal poised to strike. It's not out to get you. It is simply a combination of thoughts, feelings and physiological

symptoms, which undermine your ability to function and enjoy life. One of the biggest challenges with anxiety is that it promotes an intense self-focus, leading you to constantly monitor yourself for signs of trouble. So the first step is to stop paying it so much attention. Take a deep breath and a 'so what?' approach.

- **Put away the wrestling mat.** Many people muscle up to anxiety with an 'I'll fight this, I'll get rid of it forever' approach. But going to war with anxiety is a very bad idea. It will make you tense and hyper-vigilant, which will exaggerate your symptoms – the exact opposite of what you need. Try to relax and accept your discomfort; it will allow you to think more clearly and be in a better place to use strategies to manage it.

Remember, the more attention you give your fears, the more they will cling tight and make unrealistic demands of you. So give them space but don't let them take over; there are far more productive (and fun) ways to spend your time.

How to Give a F*ck but Not Be a Sucker

A Short Guide for People Pleasers

'There are two types of people in the world,' the young woman said at her first therapy session. 'Givers and takers.'

'I want to be a giver – but I'm getting damn sick of the takers.'

She had diagnosed herself as a People Pleaser, a classic do-anything-for-anyone person, from listening to their dramas to baking cookies, and she wanted help to break the cycle.

People pleasing, despite its fame in the pop psychology world, is not a classified syndrome or disorder. It's a way of being, born of your past experiences – people pleasers are often seeking a need denied them in childhood.

This young woman had grown up in an environment where love, praise and attention were in short supply; her achievements were largely criticised, and others that were important to her were ignored.

'My mother meant well,' she said. 'But nothing was ever good enough for her. If I got a B, why wasn't it an A? If I got an A, why wasn't I first in class? If I made the basketball team, why wasn't I captain?'

The constant striving to do better had served her well at work, where she was successful, but it had fuelled an almost desperate desire for friendship, love and acceptance. More recently it was making her resentful, and she was beginning to sacrifice her own needs and health to serve others.

How To Tell If You're a People Pleaser
Here are the key signs:

- You find yourself apologising more than you should.
- You always 'go with the flow' when others suggest activities.
- You pretend to agree with others to align with them.
- When someone hurts your feelings you don't say anything.
- You give up all your 'me time' for others, even at the cost of your own serenity and health.
- You tend to adopt the views/clothing/interests of others.
- You find it hard or stressful to say no.
- You go to great lengths to avoid conflict (being around anger makes you feel stressed or anxious).
- You find it easy to give compliments but hard to receive them.
- You're always trying to anticipate others' needs.
- If others are unhappy you feel responsible and/or guilty.

- You sometimes feel resentful you are doing all the work but you don't know how to change that.
- You crave time to yourself but, in reality, you find it hard to get pleasure from your own choices.

How to Get From Too Nice to Quite Nice

My young client answered yes to almost every question. She could see her 'pleasing' had made her vulnerable to being walked all over. But she was more struck by the realisation that she'd shelved her own personality, opinions and activities to accommodate others.

'I want to give a f*ck about people,' she said, 'but I'm going to stop being a sucker.'

Here is the process to do that:

* Separate the beasts.

Recognise the difference between being kind for its own sake and doing it to keep others happy or win their approval. It's admirable to do nice things for others, but it's not healthy to need praise for your deeds or to feel guilty and empty if you don't.

* Only arseholes make cookies at midnight.

Comedian Whitney Cummings says, 'People pleasing is a form of assholery'. Grab onto her suggestion: when you go to haul the baking tray out at midnight (or any other task you resent), tell yourself you are being an arsehole. You are depriving someone of the dignity of making their own cookies. This tactic will be foreign to you at first – but it works.

* Tell them what you really (really) want.

Stop rolling over and going with the flow. Practice giving a definite answer when someone asks you what you think or what you would like to do. Sometimes you will have lost sight of what you enjoy so have a brainstorming session with yourself to reconnect.

* Do unto yourself as you would do unto others.

Look after yourself first. Pour goodies into yourself *before* you start serving the world. If your people-pleasing tank runs low, you won't be good to anyone.

* Just say no (thanks).

When you decline an offer/invitation/demand, just say no – don't add a reason or justification on the end. Actually, say 'no thanks'. Recovering People Pleasers will feel much better if they are polite.

How to Tell if You're Taking Things Too Personally (and What to Do Instead)

You've just been told your outfit sucks.

Not in so many words. But the way that woman looked at you. The way she ran her eyes the length of your body. The way she squinted at your old (but it's vintage!) jacket. You. Could. Just. Tell.

You know you shouldn't take these things personally. You should detach. Walk away. Adopt a Zen-like expression and fill your mind with clichés: seek only to control what you can control; your opinion of me matters less than my opinion of myself; what others think of me is none of my business.

Except that it is your business. You go home. You stand in front of the mirror. You recall her face. Her scorn. And suddenly this has nothing to do with her. It's all about you: your bad hair, your off-trend taste in clothes, the weight you've gained, your lumpy body, your insecurity, your self-dislike.

You have taken That Woman's Look to heart – and it hurts.

The world is a confusing place; so are the people in it. Sometimes people are mean to us. Sometimes they're not but we tell ourselves they are. Sometimes we're just too sensitive for our own good.

So here's a guide for working out the difference – and some advice for dealing with your critics.

Are You Taking Things Too Personally?
First, check your vital signs:

- You struggle to let things go. You pick conversations over and over, looking for flaws or wondering what was *really* meant.
- You are often quick to negatively judge others (it's a flow-on from being too quick to judge yourself).
- You frequently worry that you have offended someone – even when there is no real evidence for this.
- You worry excessively about what others think of you or how you were perceived in a particular setting.
- You are very tough on yourself, often questioning why other people would want to talk to or spend time with you.
- You react quickly to any form of criticism, getting emotional or defensive before you have gauged if it has any merit.
- When you reflect, you can see you overreact to small slights.
- It's hugely important to you to be approved of by other people but, even when you are, you struggle to believe it.
- You go to lengths to avoid contexts in which you may be criticised.
- When you are praised or given good feedback you feel awkward and you secretly question it.

Sneaky Ways to Deal with Your Critics
If your yes answers above dominate the rest, it might be time to thicken up your skin a little. Sensitivity is commendable but you are also living in a world where not everyone will like, or rate, you. Sometimes, too, negative feedback can be helpful – even if it doesn't feel that way.

So here are some ways to deal with your critics:

* Don't talk, don't cry.

Just do nothing. Nice, well-meaning critics will understand you are struggling with your feelings. Mean people will be disappointed because you've given them nothing to attack. If you are upset in a work setting, quietly take time out. You can ask for clarity and plan your strategy later.

* Take yourself out of the game.

Highly sensitive people tend to place themselves at the centre of their own universe. It's sad (but also wonderful) that other people are not all that interested in you. Mostly, their criticisms are the product of their own beliefs and experiences, which is worth remembering.

* Psychoanalyse THEM.

Go on, be sneaky – they won't know. Take an analytical view of the person giving the negative feedback. Their comments and the way they deliver them tell you really interesting (and often scary) things about them and the way they see the world. You might begin to see they have more troubles – and fewer friends – than you.

* Own the Truth.

Be honest about what's going on here. Check your relationship with your critic. Is this feedback being delivered with kindness? Or does this person have an agenda and/or critical history. It might be time to do a relationship stocktake. But if there's a grain of truth in the criticism, we need to face it – when we're ready. Knowing our weaknesses can give us an opportunity to grow and improve.

* Take the goodies to the bank.

Every time you deal with criticism well, every time you stop yourself from overreacting, ruminating things to death or beating up on yourself, notice it and bank it. Self-investment is the best deposit of all.

To Be Boring … or Not to Be

Am I boring? is a natural question to ask when you're feeling insecure.

Like when your date makes an excuse to leave early, or that person you're talking to at the party keeps looking over your shoulder, or there's an empty seat next to you at the office Christmas lunch.

Or when you struggle with social anxiety, which makes you fret about what you're going to say at a social event (or avoid it altogether), critique all your comments and worry no-one wants to be your friend – all of which can be isolating and distressing.

While it's normal to have some doubts over your own 'wow' factor (anyone who doesn't is unusual), it's also important to build your social skills – being able to have an easy, two-way conversation is the bedrock of social skill and a game changer in relationships. Social skill is about making the other person feel interesting or worthwhile, in whatever form it takes – and hoping something comes back the other way.

So here's a test to keep an eye on your boringness and some ideas for making yourself (slightly) more exciting.

Are You Boring?
Do you (answer yes or no):

- Interrupt, talk over people, have to finish your sentence at all costs – you might be entertaining but this style brands you as highly opinionated, dogmatic, even arrogant. Shut up for a while and sip your drink.

- Tell stories that are just a little too long – you'll know this by the glazed eyes opposite as long as you are not too busy listening to yourself to look at them.
- Never say *anything* – if you're shy or socially anxious you may think you have nothing worthwhile to say and critique yourself to pieces. You are just as worthy as everyone else, so get in the game. Start with asking one genuine question, then follow up on the answer.
- Make erratic eye contact – not holding eye contact screams I can't wait to be somewhere else. Or that you're out to steal someone's bag.
- Talk about yourself constantly – obviously. Sigh.
- Grab anything the other person says as an opportunity to insert more about yourself. Extremely common, this is the way many – if not most – conversations flow. So if you ask a question, pay attention to the answer and respond appropriately, instead of interjecting with more finery about you-know-who.
- Ask dull questions or no questions of the other person. Dull questions are better than none; asking nothing is unacceptable. We are all guilty of being boring, sometimes. So we need to try harder. Or stay home. Or at least avoid networking events where your inner bore is ripe for exposure.

Results

If you answered 'yes' even once, you can do better. If all your answers were 'no', why are you still here? Please take your riveting personality away so we can focus on ourselves.

How to Make Yourself (Slightly) More Exciting

Everyone wants to be funny.

Really, we do. We won't admit it but everyone wants to be That Guy or Girl, the one who can crack people up with a sharp one-liner. This is not (necessarily) fuelled by a desire to forge a stand-up comedy career, but because being able to make people laugh gives the impression you are socially skilled, cool to be around, loving life, *popular*.

While it's true that being funny can boost your popularity, striving to be popular is a dumb goal. Striving to be anything you're not in order to get something you want is a dumb goal.

But there's nothing wrong with trying to be – and having – more fun. And there's everything right in trying to make life lighter and sweeter for the people in your world.

Here's how to be (slightly) more exciting:

* Make your goals spicy.

Check what you're aiming for this month, this year and in life. If your goals make you feel tired and bored then you're probably tired and bored with life and tired and boring to be with. Throw out the list and make a new one full of things that light you up.

* Drop the cool act.

If your reason for getting up is to post air-brushed selfies and keep everything you say and do lined up with your Personal Brand, go away, you're making us yawn. Don't take yourself so seriously. You are not as cool as you think – no-one is.

* Tell stories but know when to stop.

Telling a great story will make you a people magnet. Not knowing when to stop will make you people-repellent. Be aware of the difference.

* Hide your phone from yourself.

Visible phones give others the impression you'd rather be somewhere else. Or you're waiting for someone cooler to call. We're all guilty of this but once you get over your offline angst, being phone-free will help you stay in the moment.

* Initiate something. ANYTHING.

Get off the couch. When was the last time you came up with a spontaneous activity for you and your partner/family/friends – then followed through on it? Surprise them and they'll look at you with fresh eyes.

* Take the muzzle off.

Voice your opinions; try hard to lock your inner critic in a cage. Even if you struggle with shyness or social anxiety, take a tiny risk. You can't get through life saying all the right things and having everyone love you – not even close – so get in the game now.

* Screw with your routines.

Don't be and do same old, same old, every day. Change it up. Enough said.

* Do (or try) interesting things.

It will give you interesting things to talk about. It will give people something to ask you about. Mostly, it will give you more investment in your own life – and that excitement will radiate through you.

* Take a conversation somewhere.

Be curious. When talking to someone, wait for their response and take it somewhere that relates to *them*. Then do it again. All roads shouldn't lead back to yourself.

* Smile.

I know, being told to smile is patronising. But when you see someone laughing and smiling in the world it's human nature to want a piece of that. Also, smiling is very, very easy. Why not do the simple stuff first?

***

Although our Busy as F*ck struggles are many and varied, the most common reasons for distress are *work*, *relationships* and our *bodies*. It's time to explore the Big Three in their many disguises, with tools and tips to help.

What Do You Do?

Mel, a digital media journalist, is seeking stress-management strategies, she says, before she 'goes mad'.

She has been promoted to a managerial role, with responsibility for five staff: she has never managed staff. She describes one of the women on her team as 'toxic' and has no idea how to handle her.

'I wanted the job but I wasn't prepared for all these personal issues,' she says. 'I feel more like a counsellor than a journalist – and I'm not a very good one. I don't get to chase and write stories anymore, which is why I went into journalism in the first place.'

Her boss, she says, is even busier than her. 'He's nearly always on the phone. When I ask for advice he looks at me like he's not sure who I am and asks me to repeat myself or asks me to send him an email to remind him. I get it, news is 24/7 now. There's no let-up. We've all got too much to do.'

Mel also reports high stress on the home front. She and her partner, Sammi, have a two-year-old son, Oli. Mel is the family's primary earner so the boost to her salary with the promotion has been welcome. But her increased hours means Sammi, who is a contract worker, has to carry a greater load with their son and she isn't coping particularly well. To add to the mix, Oli has a chronic health condition that needs extra care and Mel's mother, who lives across town, recently broke her hip, so Mel feels she needs to visit more often.

'I feel so guilty. I'm failing in all directions – as a manager, as a partner, mum and daughter. And I haven't got a second to myself to go to the gym or see friends. Something's going to give and I'm scared it's my sanity.'

Mel says if she's honest, her problems were around before she and Sammi had their son. She's always been a worrier, and now she has a whole lot more reasons to feel guilty. She also has a huge capacity for hard work, which has helped her get through – until now. She's been ignoring the signs of stress overload: she hasn't slept properly for a long time, her eating is all over the place; she has tried to ignore the rumbling unease that never leaves her. 'I'm quite tough; I just keep going and going,' she says. 'But since I took the new role it's really starting to get to me.'

Six months into her new job, Mel has started to dread Mondays. She knows she'll be greeted by another round of staff problems, and while she grapples with them, her inbox swells with messages she has no time to monitor and her phone fills with voicemails from people she doesn't have time to get back to. 'I'm constantly putting out fires and letting people down. It's exhausting.'

At home she is distracted and edgy, irritable all the time, constantly checking her phone and feeling her nerves frazzle each time a new message pings in. After they get Oli to bed, she pulls out her laptop and tries to catch up on the day's work. Often she is still folding laundry at midnight. The weekends bring no relief. 'It's bad for our family and it's bad for my relationship with Sammi but I want and need to work. I can't see a way out just now.'

'This is not how I want to be. How can I change it?'

***

Mel's personality indicates traits of a denialist. She has worked herself to burnout before putting her hand up for help. And, even then, she would never have seen a therapist if her partner hadn't insisted on it. But she now admits she's struggling. In trying to do it all, she has become physically exhausted, highly anxious and battling to focus on any one thing. She has no time to nurture herself and it's putting her at risk emotionally and physically – as well as eating away at her key relationships.

Her story is typical of the struggle so many have to meet the twin demands of work and home. And she has the support of a partner – a growing number of people are juggling work–life balls on their own. While the blurring of gender roles has led to more flexibility around work hours, earning capacity and childcare arrangements, it has also subtly increased the pressure on families. Having the freedom to 'do it all' means we now feel obliged to try, which stirs feelings of guilt and inadequacy. For many families, money is a life support unit; two incomes are necessary for survival, which means everyone's working, often long hours or shifts. For those who are just keeping their heads above water, one tiny blip in carefully laid plans can tip the balance – and not in a good way. The negative impact on families, and relationships, can be significant.

Mel's elevation to a new role – admittedly one she wanted – has taken her from the normality of 'rushed and stressed' into the warning zone. A key player in this is her new responsibility for staff, which was a key component of our work: how to manage people, especially difficult ones. But first we needed to address her stress and anxiety levels.

Just Another Manic Monday

What do you do? could be the most commonly asked question in the world. That might be because of the Big Three things that people struggle with – relationships, bodies and work – work is the easiest one to talk about. Would you ask someone you'd just met about the state of their relationship? Or what they think of their body?

People always want to talk about work, especially when our lives are Busy as F*ck, because it's often the tipping point. Work is central to what makes us content (or not) because we use it to meet so many needs: an outlet for our talents and skills, a source of income, a measure of success, a beacon of pride, a badge of identity. And if you don't believe that, try being at a party when you can't find work, have lost your job, are ashamed of what you do or have just spent the past 10 years raising kids. You either don't have much to say – or no-one has much to say to you. Even if you have the world's greatest personality, most people won't hang around long enough to find out.

Work also consumes so much of our time. We spend a third of our adult lives at work; we work years longer than previous generations, often well into our 60s and 70s. It means the workforce contains not only every personality type imaginable, but several generations side by side, which can lead to clashes in values and perspectives. Throw in the fact that work forces us to spend way too much time with people we don't like (or like too much), and that our devices keep us permanently on the clock, and you have quite a cocktail.

There are so many ways it can all go wrong.

**

Work stress is endemic: 40% of the workforce are said to struggle with stress, and related sick leave figures are steadily rising. We don't just keep our stress at work either: we take it home, where it chews up our evenings, weekends, relationships and parenting. So it has a secondary fallout: listening to your partner offload their work problems night after night will gradually wear you down, make you resent his or her employer and screw you up about a job you don't even do.

We are now being told to plan for five or six careers in our lifetimes, and at least 15 job changes. If that's true, it's unlikely all will go smoothly – and in an upward direction. It is more likely we will endure multiple restructures or 're-orgs', lose several jobs, struggle to find new ones, be pushed sideways or passed over and wade through long, intense periods of job dissatisfaction. Then comes retirement and all that goes with it: the loss of our working identities, adjustment to the invisibility of old age, less money and a whole lot more free time.

On top of all that, there are people problems. Everywhere.

People-related work stress probably trumps everything else. Power plays rear up in multiple directions: up, down and sideways. Bullying, sexual harassment, mental health issues, difficult and toxic employees, conflicts between colleagues, clandestine affairs and all the other things employment lawyers have to deal with after office Christmas parties – the range is vast and unpredictable. I've seen decent, competent people so badly bullied that they have panic attacks on the way to work. I've witnessed skilled manipulators winding up the heat on unsuspecting targets. Then, when they've seen that person off, they choose their next victim. Tiny annoyances can blow into big problems when you are exposed to colleagues day after day. Like the woman next to you who laughs too loudly and too often at strangers' Facebook posts, or the man on the other side of the cubicle who lunches on canned tuna. Every day.

Many struggle with managing staff, especially when they haven't had adequate training. They take on a new role expecting a slightly harder version of what they've been doing previously so the shock realisation that people have problems – *and* want to talk about them – can hurl them sideways. *I've got people at me all day long. I'm out of my depth. I don't know what to say. I can't do a damn thing about her marriage. She wants MORE time off work. I don't have any time for my own work.*

I once saw a highly stressed middle manager who hired a bright young woman as his PA. This young woman had a beautifully presented CV, talked up a storm in her interview and quickly made friends all around the office. For three months (her trial period) she presented as the best hire ever made. But as soon as the permanent contract was locked down, she changed. She did no work at all, took 90-minute lunch breaks and constantly took time off for hair, medical and other appointments. When her boss called her on it she spread rumours that he was an alcoholic, that she'd found whisky bottles hidden in his desk and that he'd been drunk and inappropriate with her during a recent review meeting. The manager had an impeccable track record and these rumours had no foundation but, in a lengthy process to prove otherwise, his mental health was destroyed.

***

Another 21st-century work problem that's not easily solved is we can't get away from it. Technology keeps us there. Even if we've turned our phones off, other people haven't: they're getting rid of their stress by writing us midnight emails that will be waiting for us the next day. So it's frequently a pressure we impose on ourselves. Even if our companies don't require us to be constantly available ... well ... it's pretty easy to quickly check your emails, isn't it? Even on the beach. Besides, if you don't, there'll be 3000 in the inbox a day later.

And what about if you are *not* Busy as F*ck? What about if you take a day off and your inbox fills only with spam and memes from the guy everyone avoids? What if everyone else is having back-to-back meetings and you're not invited to any of them? Or you leave messages everywhere and no-one gets back to you? Does this mean you're out of the loop? No longer necessary? Too old? Irrelevant? A person who's lost their hunger? Bound for the trash heap – or at least another restructure process? So you rush to Do More: make more calls, send more emails, engage more (with the Right People), just so you'll get some love back. Or at least a hint someone knows you've turned up today.

In a park one day, I watched a man who didn't take his eyes off his phone as two little boys swirled around him, grabbing at his hand, chatting non-stop. It's not for me to judge, as I have no idea what's going on in his world. But it's such a common sight. In trying to perform multiple roles as managers, employees, partners, parents, siblings, friends, mentors, coaches, volunteers, we don't put our phones away. We don't know how. Perhaps, too, we *want* to stay connected. Perhaps it makes us feel important. Perhaps in our Busy as F*ck lives we need that text message, that post like, that smiley emoticon, as an escape from of the drudgery. Perhaps the high point of our day is that text from that person we shouldn't be texting. So we stay connected.

Are You (Sort of) Happy in Your Work?

Apart from their stress levels, people also want to discuss job satisfaction. *Is this really the job for me? Should I jump? When? How do I find work I truly love?*

Often they have unreasonably high expectations for their work or career: it has to tick so many boxes and, if it doesn't, then maybe it's not right for them. I recall one young woman list what she wanted from a job: intellectual challenge, a lot of money, learning, creativity, great colleagues, a supportive boss, a social life, fun, passion.

'That's quite a tall order from one source,' I said. 'Does your work really have to do all that? Is it allowed to have some boring bits like everyone else's?'

After a few seconds she began to laugh. 'No wonder I don't have a partner,' she said.

But she was right in wanting to assess her satisfaction in her current role. Here is the questionnaire I use, adapted to suit each role:

Test your Work Satisfaction

- What word best describes how I feel about my current role: Motivated? Inspired? Growing? Challenged? Bored? Overwhelmed? Anxious/stressed? Trapped?
- If I stay where I am, what will my life and career look like in one year? Five years? Ten years?
- What are my top three career aims? Challenge? Learning? Excitement? Status? Money? Contentment? Freedom? Responsibility? Stability? Creativity? Personal Growth? Work with great leaders/cool people? Other?
- Does my current role offer me these things – now and in the future?
- Am I learning new things? Are there opportunities for me to do so?
- When I walk in the door to work, do I feel enthusiastic? Energetic? Fresh? Exhausted? Filled with dread? Bored? Old/irrelevant? Out of place?
- Does my work environment suit me? Do I feel part of a team? Do I feel valuable? Am I contributing? Do I enjoy being around my co-workers and colleagues? Do I learn from them? Do they stretch or limit me?
- What are the three things I like most about my job?
- What are the three things I least like about my job?
- Can the things I dislike be resolved, and, if so, how? Do I have a plan for that?
- If they can't be resolved, am I prepared to make a change? Do my personal/financial circumstances allow it?

- Does my job suit my lifestyle and my personal goals? How important is that to me?
- What are my top three skills? Am I able to use them in this role/company?
- What work have I done in the past year that I am *really* proud of? Am I adding value in that area?
- What is my dream job/career?
- Is it realistic given my talents, skill set and interests? If so, how could I make it happen? What is the first step I could take?

Productivity and Procrastination: the Yin and Yang of Work

Productivity and procrastination intrigue me because in the past decade they have become embedded in the language of work. They've almost got a yin and yang thing going on, so they exist as inseparable but contradictory opposites. In other words, you can't be one thing without it affecting the other.

Many people who sign on for coaching will list both of these goals, often in the same sentence. It's almost as if in our Busy as F*ck worlds we've become obsessed with doing as much as we can (which equals success) and avoiding doing nothing (which equals failure).

- I want to be more productive.
- I want to stop procrastinating.

But it's interesting that productivity has been given such a positive spin and procrastination so negative, when both can be framed up either way.

Here's a more balanced way of looking at each:

Productivity

People don't ask for time management skills anymore ('that's so last decade'): they say they want to be more productive; they want productivity tools. It's driven by the idea that in a world where we have almost no time, it is critical to use what we've got well. I don't have a problem with that, but it scares me when the amount of stuff you get through every day is your key marker of success, even your personal value.

Why isn't spending a few hours hanging out with someone you really like a better use of time? But that's no longer enough – unless that person is inspiring, educating or advancing you (even better if you save time by getting all three from the same person).

I'm wary of the hype that says you need to do more to be worth more. Perhaps it's because I see the consequences of this stress, people of all ages who don't have the skills to relax (without devices, alcohol or substances), who can't turn down the mental noise. Young high achievers who are afraid to sit still for fear the world will pass them by, they'll miss an opportunity, they won't make their unique ecoprint on the planet, they'll waste their lives. That someone else will get what they want because they haven't worked hard enough – that they haven't been Productive enough.

Productivity, by definition, measures the efficiency of a production process. The ratio of all outputs to all inputs is called total productivity, which clearly has relevancy in a factory.

But when it's applied to human function, it all gets a bit weird. *What? You're not doing brain expansion exercises at 5 am? You don't have a locked-down morning routine? You don't read 235 books a year? Even when there are abbreviated, audio versions available?! You're not journaling daily and writing in your gratitude notebook? You are not open to learning every second of every day? What are you thinking?* (Subtext: *you loser*. Or often it's more subtle than that: just a notion that you could – or should – be doing more than you are, which is designed to make you feel bad and tap that old core belief: *you're not good enough).*

Don't get me wrong, I'm a diehard disciple of good use of time. Of ongoing learning, working hard, cultivating good habits and routines, and of trying to live as well, and meaningfully, as possible.

But life doesn't fit inside a purpose-built framework. A person is not a factory on legs, and shouldn't attempt to be one.

For a start, we don't know how long we've got. For most people, it is a longer journey than you think. And it can feel like a freaking eternity if you spend it doing the wrong things with the wrong people. And relationships are the thing that can mess us up most of all.

Instead of packing our days with activity, we need to think carefully about what makes us happy and excited, who we like to spend time with, how to have fulfilling relationships or what brings us serenity and meaning.

Try this test:

- Spend an hour by yourself, doing nothing much. No screens allowed but you can read, meditate or listen to music.
- Can you make it through the hour without feeling wound up, jittery and as if you're wasting time? If so, then go to the head of the class – you have a good base for managing your anxiety.
- Note: you should be able to do this for several hours but one hour is a tidy start.
- If you can't do this, hit the pause button. Ask yourself some questions: Is this the way you want to live? How you want to feel? Keyed up? Jumpy? Constantly in need of activity, company and stimulation?

Consider your lifestyle. Maybe you need to slow down? It's admirable to get lots of things done, not to fritter away time. But being able to relax, unwind and calm yourself are essential life skills too. Think about what and who really matters to you, what you would like to have achieved at the end of your life, because stories like 'Did you hear about the time I crushed a 90-page report in two days?' won't draw the crowds in the rest home. Nor will bringing up a picture of Important You hunched over your laptop sending emails.

Palliative care nurse Bronnie Ware identified the *Top Five Regrets of the Dying* (2011) as: (1) being true to yourself (rather than doing what others expected of you), (2) not working so hard, (3) having the courage to express feelings, (4) staying in touch with friends and (5) letting yourself be happier.

It's hardly necessary to point out a person's total productivity ratio never made the cut.

Procrastination

In contrast to productivity, procrastination is always loaded with negative associations and harsh self-criticism. Take a look at these comments from people I've worked with:

- 'I waste all my free time,' says a young software designer. 'I've got so many ideas but I'm too lazy to do anything with them.'
- 'I research things to death so I end up doing nothing,' says a media executive. 'I think I'm scared I'll make a mistake or miss out on something.'
- 'I want to exercise,' says a woman trying to lose weight. 'But I'm hopeless; when I get home I find a million other things to do, like pour a glass of wine.'

No one ever says: I lay in bed all day thinking creatively. I feel so much better after wasting six hours. I didn't get around to studying for my exam and it really worked for me.

All of which is at odds with the practices of many great thinkers who 'sat for ideas' (steel tycoon and philanthropist Andrew Carnegie), propped his feet on the desk and dreamed (car creator Henry Ford) fished for hours without bait (inventor Thomas Edison) or wandered aimlessly through the woods (American writer Henry David Thoreau).

The problem with procrastination

Procrastination is the overuse of delay or postponement tactics. Overuse is the key because, well, who doesn't avoid or put off things that are hard or they don't enjoy?

While procrastination does not classify as a clinical disorder, it can be a symptom of depression (along with low motivation and chronic indecision). But, more commonly, it's an anxiety-based condition that can significantly impact, even shut down, your life.

But, viewed negatively, procrastination's criminal antics don't end there. It can also steal your self-worth and serenity, because the time you spend putting things off is not traded for lying in a hammock happily sipping a pina colada; it's often spent filling you up with anxiety, guilt and shame.

Many reasons have been proffered for procrastination but, psychologically, all can be placed under the banner of *fear*. What if I fail? What if I succeed? What if I'm awful at this? What if I'm great? What if my lack of skill/knowledge is exposed? What if I don't achieve perfection? What if I'm criticised? Judged? What if I don't meet other people's expectations? What if – shock, horror – I don't meet my own?

A four-step strategy for overcoming procrastination

The first thing to consider is whether your procrastination really is the *overuse* of delay tactics. If so, getting on top of it involves figuring out *what you want or need to do* and then *regulating yourself to do it*.

Good or healthy habits are the best counter for procrastination but you can't form them overnight. Habits need to be built slowly, preferably daily. And unless you have a meaningful, high-level reason for starting a habit, you will probably struggle to sustain it.

So here's how to start:

- Choose one tiny thing you want to do or change (e.g. you want to start an exercise habit).
- Schedule it for the next day. (I'm going walking at 7 am.)
- Plan a visual cue. (Set your alarm and put your walking shoes by the bed).
- Do it. (When the alarm sounds, just *do* the activity. *Do not* ask yourself how you feel because, when a habit is still unformed, feelings will frequently overrule good intention.)

Think, Dream and DO

Remember doing nothing does not make you a bad or lazy person – in fact, if you frame it as 'time to think and dream and come up with ideas' (and you don't do it too often) it can help you be an incredibly successful one.

But if you are consciously wasting time, you need to have a serious chat with yourself. A commonly held myth is that doing something is harder than doing nothing. It's not, because the mental grief you cause yourself by wasting your time, and your precious life, is not worth it.

So how do you want to spend your day? Maybe it's time to get off the couch and go set that alarm.

Work-Life Balance is Not the Holy Grail (and What to Aim for Instead)

In our Busy as F*ck whirl, work–life balance continues to hold a hallowed place. People still talk about it in hushed whispers. It's always a keynote address at wellbeing conferences. It's still seen as the best counter to work-related stress. Frenetic people speak of it as they would a mirage in the desert. *Is that work–life balance I see in the distance? Get me to the work–life balance. If only I could have a little sip of that.*

I find it strange because work–life balance is not what people really want. We've just been conned into thinking we do. No-one aims to get to the end of their lives having achieved perfect balance between work and play, fondly remembered as a man or woman of 'great balance'. We're all just hoping that a few people will say things about our better qualities and forget about all the rest. Actually, we probably don't even care about that because we won't be there.

Work-life balance is just an arbitrary concept someone decided was the key to reducing stress. It is underpinned by the idea working less will make us happy. But the number of hours we work is only one driver of distress – and there is a lot more to finding 'happiness' than cutting back on your hours. Psychologists see many work-related traps that hurt people a whole lot more. Like how we work. What we do (and whether we like it and not being able to move on). How much we have to do. Who we work with. Who we report to. Whether they bully us. And so on.

Psychologically, it's more about *why* we work ridiculously hard: something to prove, scared of failing, perfectionist standards, a way of getting approval, prefer work to home life, my only way of feeling successful, covering up for something missing. Which are all things we need to think about.

But balance isn't our real goal. We're fooling everyone, including ourselves, when we say that. What we really want is to feel okay about the lives we have right now. We want the people we love to love us back. (Same with the people we like). We want to feel calm and optimistic. We want to feel a sense of achievement and meaning.

We want lives we (mostly) want to step into when we wake each morning, lives we feel (roughly) satisfied with at the end of the day.

But how to do it?

First, forget about aiming for work–life balance because it puts the focus on external circumstances rather than your internal state. There are times in your life when you work hard because you want to, or have to, and can. Why not? And there may be times when you don't work much (or at all) because you don't want to, or don't have to, or can't. That's fine too.

Trying to achieve work–life balance at these times is an irrelevant goal. It may also make you more stressed than if you just go with the flow.

But you do need to ask yourself three things:

- Am I obsessed with work? (because that's not healthy)
- Am I burning myself out? (because that's even worse)
- Do I have personal equilibrium? (because that is the real goal)

Here are some ways of looking at each, along with some suggested strategies:

Am I Obsessed with Work?

There are many valid reasons for immersing yourself in work. The challenge. The excitement. The creative outlet. The self-esteem spike from being hugely productive. The praise for your skill or a job well done. The antidote to anxiety. Because work is *who we are*.

But the flip side is when we live for work, we are boring. Not boring with our plans and ideas and energy – but boring because we can't switch off. We can't come down. We can't enjoy ordinary things. We can't be present with, and for, our people.

And that can seriously mess with our lives.

Being Obsessed with Work Impacts Us in Three Key Ways:

1. It dangerously loads self-identity so that what you do becomes more important than who you are. So if you suffer a major work stress or setback, lose your job, or retire without careful planning, you're in trouble.
2. It raises the risk of burnout (or chronic work stress), which develops slowly, bears a striking resemblance to mild–moderate depression and will creep insidiously into other areas of your life.
3. It threatens relationships, unless your partner has so little interest in you they don't care what you do. And it can lead to kids later describing parents as 'cold and distant' figures who preferred work over them.

Have You Crossed the Line?

Here are some questions to check, and the key warning signs of burnout – followed by the most important question of all:

Work obsession checklist

- ❏ Do I get anxious when I'm not working?
- ❏ Do I worry if I don't work hard I won't achieve my goals or fall short of everyone's expectations, including my own?
- ❏ Do I think about work when I'm not working?
- ❏ Do I work on holiday – or if I don't, I feel restless?
- ❏ Do people I love accuse me of looking vacant, of not being present?
- ❏ Do I relentlessly check emails or answer work calls/ messages outside work hours?
- ❏ Do I have difficulty delegating so I take on more tasks myself?

❑ Do I feel I have something to prove by working hard/ well?

❑ If I'm not working, do I beat myself up for being lazy or unproductive?

❑ Do I find it hard to concentrate on activities, conversations and people that don't involve work?

Am I burning out?

Burnout is difficult to separate from depression, which is the main reason it isn't a classified clinical disorder, although one of the main diagnostic manuals (the *ICD-10*) lists it as 'vital exhaustion' under the category of life management difficulties. And a few countries – Sweden is one – recognise burnout as a justifiable reason for sick leave.

Many prefer the term 'burnout' due to the stigma around depression. It's easier to tell your manager, business partner or coach you are burnt out or highly stressed because it implies you'll bounce back after a little rest – which you may not.

Burnout can strike anyone, but overwhelming workloads, long hours and excessively high expectations are common triggers. Caregivers (e.g. in medical and hospital settings, social work and counselling, elderly or disability care), emergency service workers (e.g. police, fire and rescue, paramedics) and others exposed to trauma at work are particularly vulnerable.

Because burnout develops slowly, it is often not recognised until severe. It is also hard to pin burnout solely on work because there may be other contributing factors. In fact, it is frequently a life issue (such as family, money or relationships) that tips a person struggling with work stress over the mental edge.

Most experts agree burnout shows up in three key ways. If you are worried you're heading down that track, see how you stack up.

* Physical and emotional exhaustion
You can't shake the relentless feeling of fatigue. Your body feels heavy and your mind lacks zip. Even the thought of work makes you feel tired.

* Detachment and cynicism
You feel disengaged from work and increasingly cynical or negative about your contribution or the people/profession generally.

* Falloff in performance and/or feeling ineffective
This is often the last one to show up; it's surprising how long people can function at high levels in the workplace when they are emotionally fried and physically run down.

That's Me! What Should I Do?

If the warning light is blinking, don't panic. We all experience some of these feelings when we are under the pump, overworked or just having a bad day.

But if you're heading steadily down this track, hit the pause button. While there is good professional help available for burnout and depression, there is a lot you can do to help yourself if you are able to identify your warning signs early.

Most importantly, you should have good self-care strategies in place that you refer to all the time – not just when crisis looms. But remember – doing what you can to help yourself is hugely important: reach in before you reach out.

The ONE Question You Must Ask Yourself

If your answers have got you thinking, that's healthy. But if you want to turn up the heat on yourself, front up to the question that trumps them all – the one we should all have taped to our fridge doors – the question that forces you think about how other people experience you:

Am I fun to live with?

If your answer is *'yes'*, go to the top of the class as that rare beast, a model to us all of a person who does all things well. If your answer is *'no'*, at least you're honest and you have a choice about what to do with it. Starting now.

And if you genuinely *don't know* the answer, that's okay. But you've got homework. If there's someone in your world you love, go ask them. Be prepared, though: their answer might scare you.

Do I Have Personal Equilibrium?

A more helpful aim than work–life balance is mental, emotional and physical balance: personal equilibrium – all the pieces of the pizza just the right size. When we are personally balanced we are more resilient, in much better shape to deal with problems and better equipped to make good decisions about our work – and, more broadly, our Busy as F*ck lives.

Check your personal equilibrium here (answer yes or no):

❑ Being at work feels purposeful and meaningful.
❑ What I do outside work feels purposeful and meaningful.
❑ I am generally the same person at work as I am at home (not throwing on a suit of armour or adopting some weird professional persona to impress or to cope).
❑ The people I live with, or am close to, say I am fun to be around.
❑ People enjoy working with me.

- ❏ I can relax fully when I'm not working or being productive.
- ❏ I have some worthwhile relationships at work *and* outside work.
- ❏ When I wake up I can think of at least one thing about my day that feels fun and exciting.
- ❏ I have room in my head for thoughts other than work.
- ❏ I have enough energy for all aspects of my life, including relationships.
- ❏ When I get time on my own I happily fill it – with work or leisure.
- ❏ No-one important to me has called me a work bore.
- ❏ I have ways of achieving other than work.
- ❏ I am learning, creating and growing (not just in a work sense).
- ❏ I consistently invest in my physical health (eating, sleeping, exercise).

Results

All (or mostly) yes

Ideal state is hard to achieve so don't feel bad if you didn't get Straight Ys (for 'yes'). If you are able to work hard and enjoyably – and also live well – you're on track. Well done.

All (or mostly) no

Take note because your 'yes' answers should heavily outweigh 'no'. Work as much as you like; just make sure you don't neglect your health, key relationships and personal growth and creativity – because that's what makes you fulfilled and fun to be around. *Results aside, aim to balance yourself internally. The benefits will stay with you a lot longer than work will.*

A Case of Bullying: Kathryn's Story

Kathryn is in her 40s, her own brand of corporate cool obvious from the first minute she steps into my office.

She's a lawyer, working for a large government organisation where she has been steadily on the rise for the past seven years. She has a long-term partner, no kids by choice, and is a top age-group triathlete. By her own admission, she's a driven woman.

But she has a problem: her boss. 'She's so difficult to work for,' she says. 'I can't tell if she's deliberately going after me or I'm being too sensitive. I love my work but I can't go on working for this woman.'

Kathryn, with her intelligence and poise, has never been bullied previously and seems the most unlikely of targets. So, first thing she needs is confirmation her boss *is* bullying her – and it *is* impacting her life.

What Is Bullying?

Bullying is defined as unreasonable, repeated and harmful behaviour towards another.

Studies estimate up to half of us are bullied at work. It occurs in two main categories: (1) task-related attacks (e.g. unachievable tasks, impossible deadlines, too much work) and (2) personal attacks (e.g. belittling remarks, judgment/opinions questioned, silent treatment). Most commonly, it begins with task-related attacks and morphs into personal ones.

At worst, bullying can lead to severe mental health difficulties, among them depression, trauma, anxiety and panic, emotional instability and loss of confidence. It can also show up physically, with migraines, insomnia, unexplained aches and pains and gut and weight problems.

Given men still heavily outnumber women in the upper echelons of the corporate world, women are over-represented as targets in bullying statistics. But women can also be bullies, possibly far more often than statistics reveal.

Female bullying frequently involves under-the-radar barbs: subtle put-downs, rumour spreading and social isolation. Sometimes it's about being ignored or unsupported, which is hard to prove or mount a case against.

In the most serious cases, the bully fixates on an aspect of her target's character. So she may say your work is fine, but your personality, your reputation, your interpersonal skills, your relationships – those things are Not Good Enough. In other words, *who you are* will hold you back. And, psychologically, that really hurts.

Under Attack? What to Do

Being bullied (by either gender) can be isolating as well as highly distressing. But beware of thinking of yourself as a 'victim' or succumbing to a state of helplessness. It's important to do all you can to hold onto your own power in the relationship. Here are some tips:

- **Does the behaviour fit?** Ensure what you're experiencing fits the bullying criteria. Is it unreasonable, repeated and harmful? One-off incidents and rudeness, for example, don't count.
- **Keep delivering your best work.** Bullies want you to look incompetent. Don't hand them ammunition. Working hard will also keep you busy, distracted and feeling a sense of achievement.
- **Document everything.** When you're feeling harassed it's easy to forget things or have inaccurate recall. Keeping a record will make it hard for others to say you've made things up, as well as provide evidence for what's going on.

- **Check your reactions.** Sometimes your own history can make you hypersensitive to criticism. Ask people you trust to gauge your reactions. Try to stay calm: bullies want to see you upset and distressed; that's their fodder.
- **Find out about the bully's history.** Have others left (unhappily) from this department? If so, it will validate your feelings and position.
- **Ask for help.** Report your difficulties to Human Resources or people designated to help you. Go armed with documentation and proof to strengthen your case.
- **Support and self-care.** Have people outside work to support and encourage you to look after yourself with good food, sleep, exercise and social engagement. Seek professional help if you are really struggling.
- **Explore your options.** Are you in a position to leave? Could you move departments or sectors? Sometimes being bullied signals time for a change, and fresh pastures may be very best thing for you.

It's Not (All) About You

You don't have to take the blame for someone else's bad behaviour. Although it can be hard to see when you are under attack, being bullied is less about you and more about the bully's drive to position themselves.

Finally, if you are aware of bullying in your workplace, support the target and find a way to make some noise. People who make work unpleasant for others – or worse, destroy their mental health – need to be stopped.

Who's In Your Corner
(and Who's Not)?

Tom and Teina had created the archetypal blended family.

They were both in their 40s, a striking couple you couldn't fail to notice as they went about their ordinary business: tall, athletic, attractive, sociable. They'd met at a party a year earlier and within days were immersed in a passionate affair. Both were a couple of years post-divorce and single, so there was no drama with ex-partners. But there were kids – six of them between them, aged between eight and 16.

Tom and Teina believed strongly in marriage, even though their first marriages hadn't worked out – hers to a navy man had been cold and critical, his to a woman he described as stormy, with violent and unpredictable mood swings. So when they met neither could believe their luck: she loved that he was easygoing and generous with praise; he was attracted to her emotional consistency and stability. They married before moving in together, with all the support of their respective whanau and children.

Everything seemed perfect – until they set up house and realised they'd failed to square off one thing: their parenting styles.

It was a very big thing to neglect because parenting, along with sex and money, is one of the three serious conflicts for couples. Throw in the 'new wave' difficulties of blending families, the division of chores, Busy as F*ck lifestyles and the distractions (and temptations) of social media and you have a seriously challenging package.

Tom and Teina's parenting styles sat at extreme, and opposing, ends of the scale. Teina's was more authoritarian: she was highly organised and ran the household with military precision; Tom was laid-back, permissive and of the 'kids will be kids' school of thought. While her kids loaded the dishwasher, his lay on the couch watching Netflix. When she tried to discipline his kids, they lashed back with 'you're not my mother' and he defended them, saying she was too strict. When he wanted to let things slide, she was outraged at the unfairness of it on her kids – but also that he would want to raise his kids to be lazy and selfish.

It was the only thing they argued about, but the conflict was fierce and constantly brewing beneath the surface. In the nine months they'd lived together, the clashes had escalated and it now took very little to trigger a fight. Both knew second marriages were at higher risk of divorce, especially with the added complications of blending families. They were also devastated their high expectations of happiness were already falling short.

An implosion loomed, and they'd landed in therapy almost frightened at the speed with which their great romance had unravelled.

'What are we going to do?' Teina said, clutching Tom's hand. 'We love each other and we want to be together, but this is beyond funny. Way beyond. I don't know if I can do this.'

Tom agreed. 'We probably moved too fast,' he said. 'I don't know if we can ever agree on this. I wouldn't know where to start.'

Relationships: From Joy to Heartbreak (and Back Again)

What they had discovered, all too quickly, was while people can be our greatest joy, they can also fuel our biggest heartaches. While neither demonstrated a vulnerable personality style as individuals, the dynamic between them was fractured, almost to breaking point. In their favour was they'd put their hands up early for help: studies indicate only about a quarter of couples who need – or could benefit from – relationship therapy seek it. And after the early signs of trouble they wait an average of six years before signing up, which means problems have often become deeply embedded.

While they had grown up in different cultures – Tom was Pakeha and Teina was from a large Pacific Island family – both described disciplined, at times physically violent, households. But while Tom rejected the 'rule by force' parenting style favoured by his parents, Teina could see the merit in hers (as well as the disadvantages). 'My parents were too hard on us … but they had a lot of kids and were under a lot of stress. A bit like us.'

It's often said that opposites attract, but that's misguided. Any two people, or character types, can be passionately drawn together – but trouble brews when you have a clash of interactive styles, belief systems or values – especially over kids, money or sex. So the first step for Tom and Teina was to see if they could draw their beliefs and values around parenting closer – or at least find some middle ground. Because they so badly wanted to stay together, they were willing to give it a go.

Incompatibility doesn't just show up in intimate relationships; our people – mothers, fathers, siblings, children, friends, work bosses and colleagues – can all lift us up or take us down, sometimes swiftly and painfully. And as our lives get busier, and our minds more distracted, we're even more at risk of rifts, or wreckage, in relationships that matter.

We all have relationship problems. Everyone wants to talk about their relationships. Sometimes they come to therapy with that exact purpose: *how can I fix, improve, resurrect, boundary or end a relationship?* Other times, it's not the first thing they offer up, but it'll be there, hiding, lurking, waiting for its moment. And if that moment doesn't come naturally, it will rip the curtain back and reveal itself. *Hello! Here I am. We need to talk about me.*

So we do.

In working with someone you have to know the people close to them. Not personally, usually, but you need to know something of who they love and live with, how their family is set up, who they're closest to and who they're not, who they turn to for comfort and who they run from – or should. You hear reams of information about people you will never meet, including things that would horrify them if they knew you knew. Luckily, we're never telling.

I draw diagrams of families: circles for women, squares for men, bold parallel lines for couples who've split up, crosses for death, dotted lines for adoptions, squiggles for blended families, circles around who lives together, jagged lines for difficult relationships and so on. We were taught the basics of this when training but over time it's developed into a pictorial shorthand only I can understand.

These pictures are my own little drop of proof that the world is growing more complicated. Perhaps I'm imagining it, but the webs of people's relationships seem increasingly tangled, with breakdowns and blends and sliding scales of gender and sexuality. I know relationship complexities have been there since the beginning of time, but I can't help thinking my drawing is more labyrinth-like than 10 years ago.

When I tell clients I'm drawing a picture of their family, they willingly offer the details. Some just laugh. 'You'll spend the whole hour drawing,' they say, and they're only marginally joking. One woman's family complications meant I had to join two full pages together. She loved my confusion. 'Don't say you weren't warned,' she said.

What I've come to realise is the ways in which people see, function, navigate, interact and cope with the world are innumerable. Who people love, detest, want to be with and need never to be near is so unpredictable. Just when you think you have seen, and heard, it all you will be slapped in the face with a reminder that you haven't – not even close. Someone will walk in the door with a story that pricks something behind your eyelids and you'll be back at your first day in People School with your L-plates on.

Hearts can be broken in so many ways. By your mother who repeatedly locked you in the woodshed, by your father who ignored you because he was distracted by his work and the family he had hidden in another town. By parents who were so wrapped up in each other they didn't even notice you. By your lover, by someone you loved who barely knew you existed, by someone you thought was your lover but was loving someone else. By someone who left you, not by intent, but by dying. By the baby you longed for who never showed up. By the friend who betrayed you. Or the stranger who abused you. By someone you trusted who did the same thing.

But hearts can also be mended, stitched up, smoothed over and regenerated in ways that astound you and – just when you need it – remind you of the power of love.

What's Love Got to Do with It?

I was chatting to a friend one evening after she'd spent the day trying to comfort her 19-year-old daughter, who'd been dumped without warning by her first serious boyfriend.

'Relationships lie at the base of all pain,' I heard myself say. Weird. It sounded pompous in a social setting.

'Wait!' she said. 'Say that again.'

As she thought about it, I could see her running her own relationships through her mind – those she had with her parents, her siblings, her friends – the people she'd loved, left, fallen out with over time. 'So bloody true,' she said.

Relationships matter because they are fundamental to our happiness – every emotion, really. Numerous studies have linked warm, healthy relationships, and even tiny positive daily connections, with better physical and emotional wellbeing. Think about it: when we're at our happiest or most content, our key relationships are usually in good shape. And, sadly, the opposite applies. When we are struggling, it can frequently be tracked to pain in a relationship – hurt, conflict or worry about someone close to us.

Even when people cite other reasons for their struggles, a toxic or hurtful relationship often bubbles underneath it.

So it's important to invest in the right people; hold onto, and build, a handful of relationships that will last – that grow and change with you – and let the toxic ones go.

But how to do that? How do you figure out who's worth what? How do you stop being wound up/hurt/distressed/mad/distracted (take your pick) by people who don't matter?

Stocktake your relationships, that's how. Here are two of my favourite tools to help: The Pyramid and the Friendship Circle.

The Pyramid

A Life-Changing Tool for Working Out Who Matters (and Who Doesn't)

The Pyramid has you rank the people in your world. Go on, do it – from top to bottom. The only rule is that you have to put yourself at the top because you matter most – the logic is that if you don't invest in yourself first you won't be good for anyone else.

Also, don't let anyone see you do this exercise: it's a troublemaker.

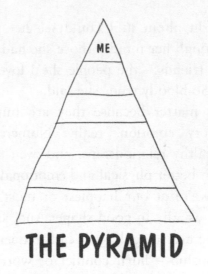

THE PYRAMID

Here are two (unrelated) examples:

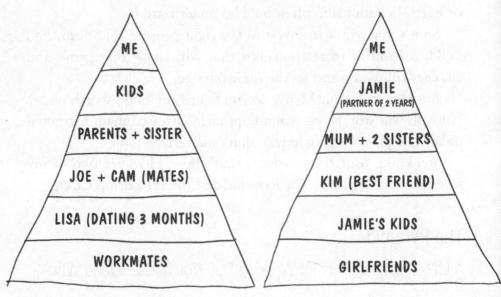

1. Mike: a 45-year-old man who has been separated for three years and has two teenaged children. He has recently begun dating.

2. Adine: a 36-year-old woman who is stepmum to her partner's young children.

Back to you. As you fill in each layer you will find that a lot of distress comes from *people who don't really matter*. For example, a lazy colleague, the bullying boss you will move on from, that competitive bitch mother in the school playground.

It also helps to identify the pressure points in your primary relationships. So if your father is your biggest problem, ask if he is more important to you than your own partner/kids? Your brother? Your best friends? You don't have to end your relationship with him; you just have to keep it in its rightful place.

I've done this exercise with a lot of people and had some revealing responses:

- Ooops. My husband's not on the Pyramid.
- Where do I put the guy I'm having an affair with?
- But I don't have any friends to put on there.
- Why am I so stressed by a neighbour I don't even like?
- My wife cheated with my best mate, so that's two I don't need to put on there.

Wait! There's More

The Pyramid also helps you work out what (or who) to say yes/no to. Here's how: when you are asked to do something, ask this:

- Do I want to do this/does it appeal to me? If the answer is no, it's easy. If yes, move to the next question.
- If I do this activity for this person, will it compromise any of the relationships ranked higher on the Pyramid (including the time I set aside for my own mental and physical wellbeing)? If your answer is no, go right ahead. If yes, don't say you weren't warned.

The Pyramid Moves and Breathes

Naturally, some of the people in your world change and move on. So it is with this Pyramid; unlike the ancient structures, it's not set in stone. Your people rankings may shift as relationships grow, evolve or fall away, or with changing circumstances or life stages.

The key is not to spend too much energy on people who don't matter, and not to compromise those who do. Nurture the good, let go of the bad. And keep an open mind (and a space on your Pyramid) for new friends. You meet some great people in the school playground too.

The Friendship Circle

People who put a lot into their friendships are often shy about putting their own hands up for support: the switch in roles can make them feel vulnerable, even weak. But that can mean they collect emotionally draining 'friends' at the expense of those who can appropriately be there for them.

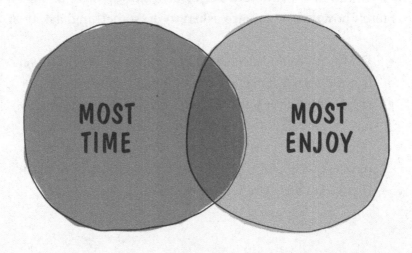

MY PEOPLE

MOST TIME

MOST ENJOY

How to 'Stocktake' Your Relationships

This is a simple way to check your key relationships, your position within them and whether they are working for you. Fill in each of the circles below with: 1) the people you spend the most time with; and 2) those you most enjoy (because they support, inspire, give you a laugh, share your interests, or whatever reason).

How Did You Do?

Obviously, the best scenario is a big overlap between the circles: that is, you spend lots of time with your favourite people. However we often find ourselves devoting more time and energy to people who make high demands of us, leaving little time for those we *choose* to be with, who inspire and uplift us.

What Makes a Friend?

In an ideal world we each have a few people in the enjoyment circle – and we make time for them. But friendships change, as do our needs. Twists and turns in our lives mean we are at times better placed to give to others too. And no-one is perfect (beware those who believe they are); we all have times when we don't show up as often or well as we can for our people.

But here's what to look for in a friend (and what to give back):

- Someone who calls when they know you are going through a hard time. More than once.
- Gives you space to be with other people (and doesn't get jealous and weird when you do).
- Prioritises time for you. And when they book you in, they don't repeatedly cancel or reschedule.
- Trust. Obviously.
- Says any 'bad stuff' to your face, not behind your back.
- Helps you pursue your goals when there's nothing in it for them.

- You *look forward* to seeing them, not like it's an endurance test for which you need to dress in combat fatigues and pre-plan your exit.
- After catching up you come home energised and upbeat, not like you need headache drugs and a lie-down.

***

US entrepreneur Jim Rohn suggests we are each 'the average of the five people you spend the most time with.'

If that's true, it's a good idea to keep an eye on the people you spend the most time with – you won't (necessarily) turn into them, and you don't (necessarily) have to cut old ties and run, but look for a balance.

It's asking for trouble to target people you want as friends – not everyone will like you as much as you like them. Instead, aim to be the kind of person you would put in your own enjoyment circle. That might be the biggest win of all.

Couples: Two-Way Love

Therapeutic work with couples is challenging simply because you are navigating two sets of thoughts, feelings and behaviours – not one.

And, most times, when a couple walks through your door one is not liking the other. More than that, the relationship is often teetering on a knife-edge and your job is to confiscate the knife and place it back in the drawer.

When a couple is 'at war', like Tom and Teina, it doesn't mean there's no love between them. Often there's great love – or at least attraction – but the whole dynamic has gotten so screwed up they can barely sit in the same room. I've witnessed anger, tears, silence, sulking, shouting – and that's while people are holding hands.

146

While not a specialist in couples therapy, I've worked with a lot of relationship difficulties, as that's the nature of being in general practice. Sometimes you'll see two people as partners: heterosexual, gay and lesbian, polyamorous. Other times it may be a mother and daughter who are fighting. Once I saw twins who were inseparable but their competitiveness was ripping them apart. You also get family disputes that can't be resolved without a mediator. Blended families and new partners can be the catalyst for vicious arguments over wills and property.

The only rule is you have to start with an even hand.

People I've seen individually sometimes ask if they can bring their partner in to work on their relationship. That's not possible: when you work with couples it's critical to meet, and engage, with both at the same time. Otherwise you're setting yourself up for an entirely justified accusation of bias.

But even meeting couples together can be fraught. Sometimes one has been dragged to therapy by the other so you have to drag the chip of resentment off their shoulder before you begin. Sometimes people have been so hurt by their partner's behaviour they are unable to articulate their side of the story. Sometimes people who've done all the hurting do all the talking too. Sometimes you feel more like a rugby referee than a psychologist.

But it's also fascinating because you get to see a micro-shot of whatever's going on at home played out in the therapy room. People struggle to hide their feelings in couples work: if even one party wants to play it cool or stay quiet, the other will call them out. Ingrained personality traits, along with past hurt, can play up dramatically in intimate relationships. One man I saw presented as open and amiable until I pressed what was obviously a hot-button for him. He sharply transferred his narcissistic relationship behaviour to me – sulking, stonewalling, bubbling aggression – while his wife sat beside him. It was almost scary to witness both

147

the speed of change and his simmering rage, but it offered valuable evidence for what his wife had described.

Narcissistic behaviour is more often reported than seen. That could be because narcissists are both superficially charming and don't think they can improve; they'll send their partner to therapy to be 'fixed', or come for a single session to give their side of the story. While disclosures of physical violence are rare in private practice, emotional abuse is common. Sometimes it's of the low-key variety, such as the woman who hated sports and kept finding ways to keep her sports-loving partner away from it, when it was the only way he kept up with his friends. Other times it comes via subtle suggestions to change yourself – lose weight, speak up, read more (to be more intelligent), wear different clothes, get new friends – which stealthily undermine confidence. Sometimes we go straight to the top shelf, where the dynamics are the emotional equivalent of a car crash.

Men are victims of emotional abuse too – and the numbers may be significantly higher than thought because it often goes unreported. Men can suffer silently because they often have no idea what fits within the range of acceptable behaviour, as they tend not to confide in their mates or brothers.

I saw a man who had been ordered to therapy by his wife. She said he needed to 'sort himself out' if he wanted to be with her. He described being subjected to such vitriol, screaming, swinging moods and physical violence over nearly a decade. I was surprised he could get into work every day. He said he thought the relationship 'wasn't quite right' but added, 'Don't all marriages go through rocky patches?' He was surprised to find he had grounds to – and should – leave her. In fact, I was worried about his depressive symptoms, which were steadily getting worse. But, stuck in a cycle of love addiction and abuse – and worried about the fate of his still young sons – he couldn't do it. 'Not yet,' he kept saying as his mental health waned.

Hearing, and in some cases seeing, these conflicts causes you to wonder how people ever got together in the first place. I know the answer, though. When love kicks off we're presenting our best selves; we're doing all we can to meet the other person's needs. But when the gloss fades and we see our partners as human, we turn back into ourselves. Ultimately, we want our own needs met more than we want to serve someone else's and that's when trouble sneaks under the welcome mat. Wild romance, deep love, can go horribly wrong, sometimes due to tragic circumstances – or other people. Sometimes there's a base incompatibility that makes you wish you could have run a warrant of relationship fitness before they sealed the deal. *Are you a spender or a saver? How much time do you want/need to spend with your friends? What's your view on raising kids? How do you want to split the chores?* These all seem like obvious questions but, in the throes of love (or sex), people often don't ask them.

Couples can land in trouble because one or both repeat dysfunctional patterns from earlier relationships. I recall a man raised by an aloof, critical mother who had lugged his full defensive artillery into his second marriage. His first marriage had broken up for the same reason. Every time his new wife made a minor suggestion about what to do or how to do it he went into orbit because he needed to be right in order to feel valuable. He wanted to change and he tried hard, but he kept putting up the shield, which was shutting down her own emotional expression: her fear of his unreasonable reactions was causing her to become quiet and withdrawn.

People often ask if you can tell which couples are going to make it. You can't be entirely sure because you can't predict people's tolerance levels, nor the external factors that combine to keep them together. One couple stayed together to look after their chronically ill dog. When the dog died they had nothing to bind them and they grew more and more distant until they broke up. But you can predict quite accurately (and quickly) whether a couple has any shot at happiness together, or at least finding a comfortable, functional space between them.

Research such as that from Drs John and Julie Gottman's Love Lab suggests a show of contempt is the breaking point in relationships. Once a person decides the other is worthless, or beneath all consideration, there's no going back. That both makes sense and holds true in therapy.

A more subtle clue to demise is the inability to see a partner's viewpoint. Some people are really good at faking it in sessions, but it always shows up in one way or another. I recall a woman unable to apologise to her partner for cheating, even though she admitted she'd been with two other men. When he explained his sadness, and broke down in the face of it, she searched out ways to justify her behaviour that didn't make sense. It was a lesson to me, as even though she was intelligent in an academic sense, and wanted to stay with him, her emotional understanding was severely stunted. While it undoubtedly had roots in her traumatic childhood, that didn't make his experience of her any easier to tolerate.

They stayed together in the short term but, if it had been ethical, I would have told him to go home, pack his clothes and buy an air ticket.

It seems to me if you genuinely can't see things (even slightly) from your partner's perspective, then you are lost, because as soon as there's a dispute you automatically hold fast to your position. And this is a mighty barrier to progress and change.

It's true of the world too. If we could all see another perspective, wouldn't it spare us so much conflict?

Not Only the Lonely

Loneliness is a silent presence in therapy. Few people reach out solely because they are lonely, even though it may be at the core of their distress. While not a clinical disorder, therapists are always keeping an eye out for loneliness, as it has a significant psychological impact.

Most of us will feel the burn of loneliness over a lifetime. It's normal to feel lonely when circumstances change abruptly, such as with the death of a partner, a relationship break-up, a move to a new country or city, or exclusion from a friendship group or social event. These symptoms, which show up as an adjustment disorder or mild depression, can last 6–12 months before they begin to dissolve. Some take longer; that's normal too.

But chronic loneliness is another matter: long-term sadness and emptiness can leave a serious imprint on our lives. It can begin with abrupt change or loss, but it can also be insidious, stealing into once close relationships as couples draw apart. A lot of loneliness happens inside relationships, when people feel they've lost that deep connection with their partner. Over time, and in the great wash of ordinary life, hopes and dreams are buried, joint planning stops, once fun and interesting conversations turn into nothing more than transactions: *Your sister wants you to call her. Have you paid the phone bill? Toby needs new shoes. Can you pick Sophie up from soccer practice? The wi-fi connection's gone down.*

We begin to fall into routines that promote emotional distance: one person watches reality TV while the other scrolls through their phone; one likes to turn in early, the other is a committed 'night person'. So we grow distant, sex diminishes, we lose the affection but hold onto the relationship, often out of a fear of being alone but, in doing so, doom ourselves to the disconnection we are trying to avoid.

People want to be connected; more than anything they want to feel someone cares for, and about, them. Sometimes we confuse wanting to feel loved with wanting to have a partner, because one does not necessarily lead to the other, and having a partner is neither a predictor of happiness nor an antidote for loneliness.

I have seen people 'in love' who are utterly miserable and people with no-one at all who are enviably content. I have seen people with toxic partners they can't stay away from and people who have wonderful partners but keep one foot dangling over the fence. I have seen people who will struggle to find love until they can break the chains to their past – and the patterns those chains have forged. I've seen great relationships too: people who are naturally good at giving (and receiving) love, people who have gotten better with time (and effort) and people who just got lucky.

Love doesn't always present in the package you want, are seeking or expect but if your heart is open, it has a chance of finding you.

I once saw a woman who waited years for her cheating husband to return. In that time he dated promiscuously, found a girlfriend, moved in with her, got her pregnant and bought a new house. Still, his wife waited for him: 'She's not right for him. He'll be back,' she insisted, despite any evidence to support her belief.

One day she met a man and dated him in a flurry of revenge. It didn't last, mainly because he reminded her of the ex she was beginning to hate but still wanted back. But he left her with a Labrador pup she had fervently not wanted. It would be too trite to say the pup mended her heart but it gave her a target for her affections, it made her feel loved and it forced her outside her head, and her loneliness, back into the world.

Losing Love, Finding Love, Holding onto Love: Three Tools to Help

People often hold themselves to high standards in relationships – then lash out at themselves when it doesn't work out, even if it's not their fault.

A twice-divorced solo dad was struggling to understand why he had so much trouble with women. He was an engaging man, ran a highly successful plumbing business but was so down on himself because he couldn't make a relationship work.

'How many serious relationships have you had?'

'Two. My marriages.'

'So why are you expecting yourself to be good at relationships? How many pipes did you have to fix to get good at plumbing?'

He laughed in that way people do when they've just realised this therapy thing might not be a total waste of money. 'I need to do my apprenticeship then,' he said.

When people have been hurt or traumatised by love, or when they lack experience in relationships, it can be helpful to: (1) have a way of processing what happened before you get into a new relationship; and (2) establish a baseline for what you need and deserve in a partner – and what you should be looking to give back. Finally, when you are in a relationship it can be helpful to: (3) have a means of periodically checking in to see whether you are both in a fit and healthy place. Here are three tools to help:

Tool 1: When You've Been Hurt by Love

You don't have to 'fix' yourself

A recently separated man signed up for therapy: his heart hadn't just been broken, he said, it'd been smashed on the rocks.

'I'm useless at this stuff,' he said, trawling through a history of unsuccessful relationships with women. 'I need to fix myself before I go back in there.' He made 'there' sound like a beast's lair; his fear was palpable.

It's a common story. People who've been hurt in relationships often turn on themselves, decide they are utterly flawed and the work is all theirs to do. They'll come to the first session clutching an iPad or a notebook ready to attack the project that is themselves.

It's a good idea to explore hurt: it can help us understand why we think, feel and behave the way we do and it's healthy to be up for learning and change. But it also makes me nervous when people view themselves as a project. Because personal development doesn't have a deadline: you can't just close the file.

So what to do?

When your relationship breaks up, your confidence takes a hit, even when you were the minor player in all that went wrong. Not everyone wants – or can afford – therapy so, assuming it's definitely over and you've taken all measures to block a return, here's a guide to unpacking your pain.

* Wallow

Just for a little while. You're allowed. It hurts.

* There's a lot to like

What did you like about yourself in your relationship? When it's on the slide it's easy to lose yourself. And if you've been with a discontented partner, you may have spent a lot of time trying to make them happy at the expense of your own needs. So take time to write down all that you brought and gave to the relationship. If your break-up has been drawn out and gruelling, think back to when you first got together.

* Choose your words carefully.

One young woman who had not been happy with her partner insisted on saying 'I've been dumped' when they broke up. It cast her firmly as the victim – when she wasn't. While it may be true you were dumped, cheated on and had your heart broken, using those words will keep you stuck. As soon as you can, say 'we split' or refer to it as a 'broken relationship' and your partner as your 'ex'. It will help you detach from the difficult emotions.

* Tap into your insecurity.

When a relationship is rocky, all our insecurities rise to the surface and we can behave in ways foreign to us. Sometimes we over-try for a relationship we know is bad, for us or we're not even that into. Where's the logic in that? Ask yourself if your partner gave you reason to feel insecure – or was this something you created out of fear?

* Feel the déjà vu.

Be honest – have you been here before with someone else? This is perhaps the biggest clue to any difficulties you have in relationships. Even though we are with different people, we tend to play our relationships the way we always have. If the same behaviours are tripping you up, pay attention.

* Ask: would you date yourself?

Everyone behaves badly in relationships at some point, and everyone can do things a little better. But a stressed relationship and break-up can lead you to lose a grip of who you are – and what you're like to be with. So write down your biggest failing (or vulnerability) and how you could do it differently in your next relationship. If you can't think of anything you did wrong, sit there until you can.

* It's not all about you.

Honestly, perhaps your partner was wrong, even bad, for you. Perhaps he/she is not so great for anyone else either (but that's no longer your problem). Did you ignore the warning signs in your partner for far too long? Sometimes it's not all about you. The most blame you can shoulder is your choices.

Remember, you're not a project to be handed in. You're just a work in progress, like the rest of us. There is no ideal time frame for getting into a new relationship. Just ensure you don't keep dragging baggage from your previous relationships with you: the load will break your back – and your spirit.

Tool 2: When You're Looking for Love

Seven Signs Your Partner Is Good Enough for You (or What You Deserve in a Relationship)

A young man couldn't find a girlfriend. He dated lots of women but none of them made it to the third date – even when she was keen, he called time on it.

Frustrated, he came up with the idea of a checklist, detailing all the things he sought in a woman. I didn't see the checklist but things like *hot, outgoing, laughs loudly at my jokes* and *great-at-sex-without-having-had-much* always rate a mention.

Each date was given points out of 10 in each category which dictated his decision to pursue her – or not.

'Do you think that's a good way to find love?' I asked, carefully avoiding words like 'shallow' and phrases like 'destined for disaster'.

He smiled back.

I didn't see him for a while after that – possibly because his social calendar was brimming – but a few weeks later he emailed to say he'd binned the checklist. 'It was dumb and a bit mean,' he said.

It was indeed dumb and a bit mean, but I wrote back kindly because he was a lovely man who'd just been carried away with all the choice the online dating world had thrown at him.

With so many options, why would he settle for average? Why wouldn't he seek perfection? Why wouldn't he wait until all the stars aligned and their souls sang together under a perfect crescent moon?

Because forever is a very long wait.

While setting the bar low in relationships is foolish, even dangerous, it's also important to be realistic in the quest for love. One person can't meet *all* your intellectual, social, sexual, emotional and spiritual needs *all* the time – nor should they; they'd have nothing left for themselves, which would make them boring to be with, not to mention miserable.

Your partner does need to be 'good enough' for you, though, according to your own standards. If you're not sure what these are, if you've lost your way after a messy break-up or if your relationship history has been hurtful or traumatic, it's important to think about what would really work for you – and your future.

What You Deserve in a Relationship

When I work with people on the other side of heartbreak we always explore what makes a good relationship so they will 'see the light' next time. We do this even though we both know that light doesn't always shine right away, that it can take years for a person to show their true worth, or their darkness, to someone else.

What surprises me is that while people experience love in so many different ways, the same things rise to the top over and over again. So here are the qualities you deserve in a partner:

- Someone kind (and who is kind to your favourite people) because mean stays mean forever. So does critical.
- Someone who is where they say they will be (and with whom) because trust (really) matters.
- Someone who can manage their emotions (within reason) because extreme ups and downs are confusing and exhausting.
- Someone who is not lazy, because there's just a lot of work to do. And who wants to come up with *all* the ideas?

- Someone who is quite fun, as you get sick of laughing at your own jokes. And, even in suffering, life should not be relentlessly grim.
- Someone who wants the same things from life as you, because diverse roads will never merge. Not happily, anyway.
- Someone who can love and support you back (this one doesn't need a reason).

And we all should remember it's not fair to insist on these things in someone else unless we can offer them back – consistently. Because your partner deserves them too.

***

A few years after working with the man with the checklist, I saw him out walking with a woman and two children, one of them a new baby he carried in a backpack. He spotted me and waved. As I walked past, the woman leaned over and helped herself to a sip from his takeout coffee. Then she reached up and ruffled his hair. I bet those things were never on the checklist.

Tool 3: When You Want to Hold On to Love

How to check your relationship's fitness

Imagine if you could take your relationship to a WoF testing station for an annual service. Run it through a checking system, patch up the conflicts, add a couple of new communication skills and get a permit that says you can stay together for another year.

If only it was that easy.

While some relationships should come with bold warnings – 'CRITICAL FAULTS' or 'STRUCTURAL WEAKNESS' – and others should be taken straight to the wrecker's yard, many are worth holding onto. There's something irreplaceable about sharing experiences with someone over a long time.

The trouble is, when there have been difficulties, we often don't know where to start: what to replace, what to fix, what to pour oil on, what tools to use. After conflict, we may cling stubbornly to our perspective because it feels like a lifeline – and that stops us from being able to see things from our partner's perspective.

So – if you're brave enough – take your relationship to the testing station. Do an honest assessment. Be truthful about your own role in it. And if you think it's worth preserving, roll up your sleeves and get to work on the things you can improve.

Some relationship inspection requirements

- **Who are you when you are with your partner?**
  What characteristics do you most exhibit when you are together? Do you like who you are within the relationship? Your relationship should enable and encourage you to be an authentic, contented version of yourself. If you don't like what you see when you stare yourself down in the mirror, something needs to change. (Note: this is self-analysis, not a blaming exercise!)
- **Do you trust your partner?** *Can they have a night out or go away for a weekend without you fearing the worst? Do you trust them with money?* If either one of you has been hurt, then hopefully you are taking steps to rebuild that trust – because it won't do it by itself. Mistrust left untended is a fire waiting for a match.
- **How do you (as a couple) handle tough times?** *Are you able to pull together and support each other? Or do you go into your own cave and let your partner fend for themselves?* It is well known that a crisis, grief and other

difficulties can crack – or even devastate – the strongest
of relationships. It's important to be able talk, to listen
to the other's view and come up with a joint strategy for
moving in the same direction.

- **Do you support your partner's independent dreams,
  goals and opportunities to have their own fun?** *Do you
  want and encourage your partner to do things without
  you? Or do you cling tight, wanting to do everything
  together?* While a few couples are happily inseparable,
  most relationships need (and grow from) time spent
  apart. Ensure you support your partner's independence
  while nurturing your own.

- **Do you have compatible values?** *Do you generally
  agree over money, religion, parenting, sex? Or are you
  constantly in dispute, tripping up over the same old
  issues?* If your values clash consistently, can you find a
  way to live easily with your partner's perspective?

- **Can you resolve conflict?** *Do you have (and use) sound
  communication and conflict resolution skills?* After a
  fight, many couples use unhealthy strategies, such as
  storming out of the house, periods of silence or acting
  'cold', withdrawing sex, until they slowly get back
  to 'normal'. It's okay to disagree as long as you have
  means of resolving disputes – and you owe it to any
  children you have to model healthy ways to get things
  back on track.

- **Do you have fun together?** If there are no easy laughs,
  if you don't look forward to some time alone with your
  partner, then do a reconnaissance. Laughter with your
  partner, or a shared in-joke, is a huge indicator of good
  relationship health. Remember, even when times are
  tough, laughter is the best medicine. Except, of course,
  when medicine is the best medicine.

So how'd you go? Does your relationship need a tweak? An overhaul? Or is it, on balance, roadworthy? If so, then jump back in the car. You might just have years of happy motoring ahead.

Relationships: Things People Ask

Commitment. Lust versus love. Cheating. Separation, conflict, communication. These are the most common relationship issues raised in therapy, with many (many) variations on those themes. Here are some strategies to help with these difficulties written in response to frequently asked questions:

My Partner Won't Commit

Q. I'm 29 years old and been with my boyfriend for four years. We still don't live together (as he doesn't want to), and every time I bring up getting married or having kids he shuts the conversation down. Am I crazy to keep waiting for him to commit?

Dear I-Want-More,
I once worked with a young woman whose boyfriend refused to marry her. She was bright and fun, with good career prospects.

When I asked her to describe him, she said he had no job, no car, no house, no decent friends. He was lazy, overweight and unfit. He was an angry drunk, smoked too many drugs and constantly put down her body and looks. He was also missing two front teeth.

Almost speechless, I managed this: 'Please at least tell me he's phenomenal in bed.'

'Not even average,' she said, laughing raucously at her desperation to be with this man. 'I must be insane.'

The point is, there is something more important at stake here than whether or not your boyfriend will commit to you. It is whether he's worth the effort.

Too often people get seduced by the idea of being in a relationship, of having someone to love, and to love them. That can override sensibility when it comes to choosing, and staying with, a partner. It can also make you desperate.

So your top priority is to make sure your desire to be with someone isn't masking some serious flaws in him. *And* that he's a consistently decent person in the world, especially to you.

If he passes this test, then make sure you have clearly and calmly stated what you want from the relationship, and the time frame in which you would like it to happen. That means having the conversation when you are not angry or upset; that means listening carefully to what he has to say, because that matters too.

So What's Commitment Phobia?

Commitment phobia generally refers to the inability to keep promises to other people, but it is most often associated with intimate relationships.

While not a clinical disorder, some people experience significant relationship anxiety. They may not be able to handle the intensity of feelings or they may crave intimacy while being unable to sustain it due to fear-based issues. These can be rooted in trauma, childhood attachment issues, abandonment, abuse or infidelity.

But whatever the reason for your partner's avoidance, you still have to consider what that behaviour means for you and your future.

Check your partner's avoidance with these questions:

- Does he say 'I love you' meaningfully?
- Does he call you his girlfriend to people (who matter)?
- Has he previously been able to commit in relationships? Or has he left a trail of short, messy ones?
- Does he often answer 'maybe' rather than 'yes' or 'no' to invitations from friends?

- Does he always show up where and when he says he will? Or is he notoriously unreliable?
- Does he make holiday or longer-term plans with you (and keep them)?
- Does he show due care to your (reasonable) wants and needs?

If your partner struggles with these basics, be warned.

Remember, there are two sets of needs in a healthy relationship. You should give and take in equal measure. Your boyfriend sounds happy with his end of the deal. So the big question you need to ask yourself is: are you happy with yours?

***

Am I in Love or Lust?

Q. There's a hot, charming guy in my group of friends who I really like. We are both single and have hooked up a couple of times. We hang out often and text a bit of banter. However, I don't want to ruin our friendship for nothing; it would mess up our group. How do I know if I am just lusting over him or if I am in love? Is there a difference? Does it even matter?

Dear Confused,

Relax, my friend. So far, so good. You've met a single man you like enough to have fun with – and that's all. Figuring out the difference between love and lust can be confusing because they often start out the same: with sparks, sexual attraction and an addictive sense of exhilaration.

But whereas lust is a strong sexual desire based on physical attraction (and therefore more vulnerable to burnout), love is founded in deep emotional attachment.

163

Let's say you're in lust right now. Your body's tingling, your heart's racing and you're high with energy and excitement. You may have lost your appetite and your mind is filled with thoughts of a virtual stranger. In other words, your physiological experience is real, but your common sense may have taken a hike.

Studies of the newly infatuated estimate up to 85% of waking hours are devoted to the new love and, with those obsessive thoughts, come compulsive behaviours (e.g. constantly checking our phones, trying to orchestrate 'natural' meetings, making ourselves ridiculously available for a date).

The danger is we're gazing at our lover through a sparkling lens, elevating their good features and dismissing any red flags – even when they're being waved under our noses.

So, best advice? Figure out what *you* want from this relationship? Do you like things as they are? Do you want to date him? Exclusively? Do your needs and expectations match his? Any kind of relationship is fine as long as you're both consenting and agree on what it means to you now – and possibly in the future.

So ask him. Not by text message. Listen carefully to his answer. Don't turn it into something you want to hear. And tell him clearly what you want and expect from the relationship. Old-fashioned, I know. But it works.

How to know if you're in love

If you decide to stay together, here are some signs of a love match. Hint: wait 6–12 months until you run this checklist, so your 'real' selves are fully on display.

- You can't wait to share the day's news with your partner. Even the boring things. But you are sensitive enough to know when they've had enough.
- You feel safe to share your feelings and be fully yourself. Like wearing paint-splattered sweatpants.

- The fun you have together far outweighs the gloomy or negative times.
- You have healthy ways of resolving conflict.
- You like your partner's personality. A lot. And you cope well with the annoying bits.
- You agree or have found an easy compromise on all the *big* issues: values, money, culture, religion, sex, family, children and the like.
- You occasionally feel a bit jealous of others in your partner's world – but not at all suspicious.
- You want your partner to achieve and do well (even when you're not). You're committed to being loving – as well as being loved.
- You support each other's independent interests and time with friends. Without racking up brownie points.

If lust is enough for you just now, that's fine. And if you do find lust and love in the same package, don't waste any more time trying to analyse it. The sunset awaits.

***

Finding Your Way Back from Hurt (Case 1)

Q. *I'm a 52-year-old woman and after 20 years of marriage my husband left me for a much younger woman. I've just heard she's pregnant! Our kids had left home and we were getting to a much easier place in our lives. Why would he do this to me? I'm in shock and desperately lonely. I don't know how to move forward.*

Dear Abandoned,

There's no accounting for the devastation that can come with this – particularly at this stage of your life. I can't read your husband's mind but let's just say he may well discover the grass on the other side of the fence is not always green – and even if it seems that way, it often quickly turns brown – especially when he's up at the crack of dawn every Sunday morning to change a nappy and watch *PAW Patrol* on repeat.

But back to you. Like any grief, the process is very individual but these are the recurring themes seen by therapists.

*Shock. Betrayal and abandonment can have a physical, as well as emotional, impact. Tears, anger, sleep and eating problems, nausea, obsessive thoughts, extreme anxiety or panic are common.

*Self-blame. Even though rejected partners know they're not responsible for the situation, they still wonder: Am I stupid? Why didn't I see that coming? What did I do wrong? Is it my age? Looks? Lack of excitement? Am I not worth more than this?

*Emotional rollercoaster. Sadness, anger, denial, resentment, revenge, fear – the emotional ride is bewildering and can rock mental stability. Experiencing these feelings is *valid* and *normal* – but when emotions are allowed to run the show for too long people become stuck and bitter. Those who can't find a way to shuffle forward should seek professional help.

*Fear of the future. Again this is expected, and can involve money worries, where and how to live, fear of being alone now and in old age. It's important to make a plan around the logistics, the things that *can* be controlled, because there will be some things that can't.

*Acceptance and rebuilding. This is the golden ticket. Once people accept their lives have changed permanently, the switch will flick. Acknowledging loss and the flaws in the ex/relationship is a key step to recovery. From here, people can move forward healthily, including being ready to love again.

Your ex-husband may eventually regret what he's lost – or he may not. His actions are not for you to analyse or understand. Your job, beyond grieving, is to shore up your dignity and make a good life for yourself, whatever it takes. And enjoy your Sunday mornings in bed, alone or not!

***

Finding Your Way Back from Hurt (Case 2)

Q. My girlfriend of four years dumped me when she met another guy. I'm 30, we were living together and planning to have a child – I thought she was the one. It's been six months now and I'm stuck; I can't stop thinking about her. I'm constantly tempted to text her. My anxiety is terrible; I'm afraid I'll bump into her every time I go out. How can I stop obsessing and move on?

Dear Stuck,

Ouch, that hurts.

People who've been cheated on can suffer mood and anxiety symptoms, similar to post-traumatic stress disorder. Sleepless nights, intrusive thoughts, thinking about what, when, how and why – asking endless questions they don't really want the answer to. There can be panic and flashbacks as they ride the emotional waves; self-esteem and trust issues can flare and take a long time to heal.

So here are a few tips to help you to the other side. And there *is* another side!

- **Delete and block.** Cut ties with your ex every way you can. People recover more quickly from emotional pain when not exposed to things that trigger related negative thoughts. If you don't have the strength to commit to that – especially drunk at 3 am – enlist your friends and download blockout tools/apps to help. Limit your time with mutual friends of your ex if possible, at least for a while. You need time and space to shuffle forward.

- **Don't cyberstalk.** It's super common and all too easy to track someone by keyboard. You especially need to impose some tough self-love if you're cross-referencing social media accounts to piece together your ex's new life or inventing online identities so you can stalk without being discovered. That's unhelpful, unhealthy – and (a bit) weird.

- **Let yourself hurt.** Being rejected stings; it's healthy to acknowledge and feel pain – but beware of wallowing. Wallowing can turn self-indulgent and will prevent you from fully engaging in the things and people that are good in your life right now.

- **Ditch the rosy glow.** A person who dumped you is a person who dumped you. Don't hand them any more power than that. Strange as it might seem, someone who rejected you was never right for you. Their own agenda would always have overridden their feelings for you.

- **Go after the flaws.** Force yourself to write a list of all the reasons you should not be with her. If you think she was perfect, wake up – everyone has a dark side and this is the one time you are allowed to go after it. Keep the list in your phone and read it aloud whenever your vulnerability kicks in.

- **Depersonalise your loss.** Recognise your heartbreak is less about losing this person and more connected to your own story: how you feel about love, loss and your own needs, desires and self-worth. If you can't process this yourself if may be worth seeking professional help so you're better equipped for your next relationship.

- **The great escape.** Instead of thinking of yourself as single and lonely, tell yourself you're free. And unhooking your future from someone who didn't want you might be your best move yet.

- **You're still here.** Plant your feet firmly on the ground. Take care of yourself. Your ex can hurt you, uproot your present, reshape your view of the future. But they can't steal your life from you. The best thing you can do is get back to living the width of your life as well as the length of it. One day at a time.
- **Great clothes don't hurt either.** Go treat yourself.

Who Gets the Kids?

Q. My partner and I separated eight months ago. We have two children, five and nine. They usually split their time between us, which is working out okay. However, this will be our first Christmas not as a family unit. My ex and I are fighting over where the kids should spend Christmas Day. It's not an option to share the day because we're too far apart. Christmas has always been special to us – how can we agree on who gets to spend it with the kids?

Dear Not-Very-Merry,

There's no way I can gift-wrap this for you – your first Christmas apart will be difficult.

Yours sounds particularly tough because the distance means it's not possible for your children to spend time with both of you.

Sadly, it's all too common. Every year we therapists are slapped with the irony of Christmas being portrayed as a time of joy and goodwill, when so many people are struggling.

Santa must have an excellent PR company.

For newly separated parents the challenges can be significant. First, there's the difficulty of making a plan with your ex-partner when you can barely tolerate speaking to them.

Throw in worries about money, blended families, new partners, jealousies, resentment, competitiveness, loneliness and you have a cocktail decidedly lacking in festive spirit.

So here are a few tips to help you get through it:

- **Lock down arrangements early.** We all know when Christmas falls, so there goes that excuse. I know it's difficult but talk to your ex about how you can make things work in the kids' best interests. Face-to-face communication is best – but whatever it takes.
- **Don't ask the kids to choose.** This is your job – in collaboration with your ex. Don't load your children with pressure they don't need. If you can't agree, seek help to do so, preferably a trusted, neutral person or a professional.
- **Be nice, not naughty.** Be fair – even if you have reasons not to be. Provided there are no safety concerns, your partner has a right to spend time with his kids, just as they have a right to be with him.
- **Prepare for tears.** Acknowledge this an emotionally charged day. You are allowed to cry – but don't burden your children with your unchecked feelings. They should not have to be your 'rock' and mop up your distress.
- **Resist spoiling kids.** Separated parents often try to compete: who can give the best presents, have the best day, etc. Don't go there. Kids may act like they can be bought but when they hit therapy years later they'll tell you they just wanted love, time and emotional consistency. Trust me.
- **Be a role model (even if you hate the idea).** Your kids are watching you: show them you are capable of carrying on – even having fun – on your own or with your own family/friends. Girls need to know women don't collapse without a man. Boys do too.
- **Structure your day.** Plan the time you have on your own carefully; include some enjoyable activities. It's fine to

miss your kids but it's also okay to have a good day without them. Share your plans with them: part of their happiness is knowing you are going to be okay too.

Finally, when the day arrives and you have a quiet moment, pour yourself a glass of your favourite tipple and toast the year you've put to bed. Separation is not easy. Well done; you're doing okay.

We Don't Talk Anymore

Q. I've been with my partner for 13 years. We niggle, we pick, we argue. The gaps between the fights are getting shorter. The silences are longer. We used to have a lot of fun together but it all seems to have dried up with time, work, kids and all the admin of life. Is this normal? How can we get back what we had?

Dear Niggles,

Firstly, know you are normal: 'we don't (or can't) talk any more' is the number one issue for couples entering therapy.

Sometimes there's been a trigger for it, like a sexual or financial betrayal or the fight to top all others. But often it's just like you say: time, life and a slow-burning disconnect. A feeling that your partner doesn't hear what you're saying – or worse, that it's selective: that he or she is not even interested.

When couples can't communicate, what they're really saying is we've lost our connection – and we have no idea how to get it back.

Sadly, you can't just talk your relationship out of trouble. Talking at length may not help you feel connected – it may even make things worse because the same old problems are endlessly raised and never fully resolved. They're just put on the backburner until someone strikes another match.

The key is to make sure you're speaking the same language, that the conversations are productive and move forward. Here (in no particular order) are the five problems that most often rear up in therapy – and some tips for easing them.

- **Fixating on an issue** – this is common when someone has cheated and the hurt partner finds it impossible to let it go. The slightest provocation or reminder can set off an argument. Tip: If you find yourself obsessing on an issue, you need a *process* and *strategies* to work through these issues. If your own reading or investigations don't hit on something that resonates, ask a professional.
- **Inability to express own needs** – it is important to say what you want and need from the relationship. Difficulties often arise when people expect their partner to have read their mind. Tip: If you have difficulty with verbal expression, or you tend to get upset, write things down before you discuss them with your partner.
- **Not being able to understand another's viewpoint** – listening is good but you have to absorb what the other person is saying and show that you have heard them through your actions as well as words. Tip: Put your phone away and look your partner in the eye when they're talking. Then come up with one thing you can *do* to show you've heard them. Actions speak (much) louder than words.
- **Attacking your partner's character over their behaviour** – 'I'd appreciate you helping with the dishes' is more likely to get a positive response than 'you're such a lazy arse'. Tip: Keep comments about negative behaviour specific to a situation or single behaviour. Sweeping generalisations can hurt and can't be taken back.
- **Emotional response that is too quick or harsh** – being overly defensive and blaming are the primary offenders. This is particularly common if you have been heavily

criticised by a parent or in other relationships. Tip: When you are upset or annoyed, it's important to hit pause and take some time out so you can consider the fairness of your response instead of acting on impulse and lashing out.

The good news is relationships can be extraordinarily resilient – sometimes they have to be! But we all need skills to deal with conflict, pain and trauma – and also just to navigate the different phases relationships go through.

Not everyone needs professional help. But consider it if you can't find a way forward yourselves. Relationship therapy is not an admission of failure. It's just like a health check. If your body was sick you'd go to the doctor. At least I hope you would. Doesn't your relationship deserve the same care?

Let Me Hear Your Body Talk

'I hate myself,' Alice says within the first minute of our meeting.

I've heard this so many times in so many ways; sadly, it's just too often a part of being female. But the extremity of Alice's self-loathing catches me off guard. It began with 'asymmetrical' facial features and ate all the way through to her core, where she says she feels empty and lost.

'I'm so ugly,' she says. 'Look at me – my face is asymmetrical. My features look like they've been thrown on. Nothing lines up.'

I try not to stare. If there is any lopsidedness in her facial structure, it's not apparent to me. But, as I had read in her GP's referral letter, it is hugely distressing to her and driving thoughts of suicide.

Alice is 32, has a science degree and works as a medical technician in a laboratory. But she flouts the white coat stereotype, turning up for our first appointment in layers of black clothing, including studded satin gloves, heavy burlesque-style makeup and shiny black Doc Martens. She has spikey bleached-white hair, with dark uppercuts shaved down both sides. She removes her jacket to reveal black and white geometric tattoos running the length of her inner arms. When she presses her arms together you can see three words threaded through them: faith, hope, love.

174

Every morning Alice spends three hours applying and reapplying her make-up, choosing and changing outfits, then if she doesn't like (or can't tolerate) what she sees in the mirror, she becomes tearful and panicky, sometimes to the point of making herself vomit, then rips off her clothes and begins again.

'You're hideous. You can't go out, you can't be seen,' the voice in her head chants. On the worst days she calls into work sick and retreats to her bed for the day. 'I can't go on like this,' she says. 'I love my job and I can't afford to lose it.'

Alice comes from a solid middle-class family; she has twin brothers 10 years younger than her whom she adores. She says she has always felt a deep inadequacy, which played out in her teenage years with friendship issues, then through an eating disorder, which saw her twice hospitalised. In her 20s, the eating problems had given way to this obsession with her face; she had even shaved off her eyebrows to give her a clean platform for correcting all the structural imbalances. It meant every day she could start afresh. 'It's the only way I can make things match,' she says.

Psychologically, I was fascinated. While body dissatisfaction is common, classic cases of body dysmorphic disorder – an obsessive belief that some aspect of the body or appearance is severely flawed and needs extreme measures to hide or fix it – are relatively rare, affecting around two per cent of people. The examples I'd read about focused on specific facial features – noses and ears – and also skin, hair, breasts and penises.

But facial features that didn't align? I had no idea how to get to the core of it until one session, by chance, I stumbled into an exploration of the other relationships in her family. Sometimes the best clues lie not in what has happened but what has not: you need to explore the gaps in the story. 'Why was there a 10-year age difference between you and your brothers?'

'After I was born my mother had several miscarriages – it made her very depressed and our house was always quiet and sad. I spent my whole life trying to make it up to her, but nothing worked. After she had the boys she got better; she said she felt normal again, back to her old self.'

I can see the link between her mother's depression and Alice's insecurity but the final piece of the puzzle remains just out of reach.

'Your brothers. What were they like as children?'

She looks at me like I'd taken far too long to get here – which I had.

'Symmetrical,' she says.

***

Body image is always up for discussion because our bodies are our shop window to the world, the physical representation of who we are – not to mention the first thing other people see. Our bodies also hold so many clues as to how we live – or have lived – and in a Busy as F*ck world that's critical information.

Alice's personality style was heavily influenced by her need for control: she could not cope with uncertainty and change of any kind – and she was convinced the solution lay in adjusting her physical appearance. While her efforts to control her inner turmoil were extreme, she was far from alone in her motivation. It's a commonly held belief that changing your physical form holds the key to a better life. Even those who don't fully believe it are often up for giving it a shot. The key to Alice's difficulties lay deeply embedded in her past and she had, over time, developed a way of coping that was now severely limiting her life. While she understood her story, she needed to be able to cope with daily life so, beyond safety issues, we began with exploring ways she could tolerate her distress and manage her emotions.

Mind and Body: Playing Nice

Alice's body anguish could be clinically classified but there are so many variations on that theme – and no wonder. Everywhere we look, there are beautiful, sculptured bodies to aspire to, bodies we wish we had or are supposed to wish we had. The online world is bursting with fit, tan, slender, buffed bodies ... or puffy, pouting lips or perky, uplifted breasts or smooth, unlined faces you can't help but envy until they try to smile.

In the past decade there's been a huge upswing in seeking psychological input for body image issues: weight, gender issues, ageing, wanting to change (or remove or add) a particular body part, adapting to the change after they've made it. It used to be people would come to therapy for other reasons and let their body dissatisfaction leak out in passing. Now they are more open. 'I've always hated my body. I'm destined to be fat. My skin is bad. My nose is too big. My eyes are too narrow. My penis is too small. My breasts are too big/small. My stomach is too flabby. I wish I was different (prettier, more toned, ripped, lighter and thinner).'

Despite healthy societal moves towards a greater acceptance of all types of bodies and related cultural differences, that's not what we see, that's not what we're bludgeoned with. Beauty in its traditional forms still rules supreme – and how we look still trumps how we think and who we are. No-one ever posts a picture of their toned mind on social media. No-one boasts about taking their mind to the gym, getting it fit, building its muscle and, when it's fatigued or injured, rehabilitating and resting it.

I wish. Mind and body are a tandem act, equal players in life quality and peak performance, so if you want to get the best from yourself you need to take your mind for a workout too; you need to give it the same strength and conditioning as your body. And you shouldn't fill it with trash either.

When I was first exposed to this idea as a young physical education student it seemed like the smartest thing I'd ever heard. Of course, it was old news even then: Greek philosophers Plato and Aristotle got there 2500 years before us, which only serves to highlight how slow we've been on the uptake.

Still, I'm a staunch mind–body advocate in my work. I add a spiritual component, too, if that works for the client, but the absolute bottom line is to have mind and body on board, aligned in their powers, heading in the same direction.

Because one will be very naughty without the other.

Not Just a Body

I've seen so few people who like their bodies I need only one hand to count them. And even then, some of them have had other agendas, such as using their bodies to get validation, approval or love. Or they're athletes who only like their bodies while they are muscled, toned, lean and doing their best work. No prizes for guessing how much that changes when they retire.

It is estimated around 70% of women don't like their physical appearance – with 'disgust' being a common description. There are no comparable figures for men, but from clinical experience, and societal messaging, it's safe to say women hugely outnumber men in their body dissatisfaction. It would be naive, though, to pretend that male numbers aren't increasing, particularly among young men who face societal (and online) pressure to be bigger and more ripped – which is contributing to the rise in steroid use among male gym users. Expect this to get worse, too, given many men thrive on competition and use comparisons to measure success. And human insecurities are not confined to women.

With body dissatisfaction the norm, I more clearly remember those who didn't care. One slightly out-of-shape young man looked puzzled when I asked how he felt about his physical self. He just shrugged.

'Okay, I guess. It's just a body,' he said. I wanted to bottle his self-acceptance.

Because for so many, it's not just a body.

I've seen the emotional pain caused by unruly bodies, bodies that won't play by the rules society – or even their owners – have set down for them. I've seen the lengths, pain and expense people have gone to change their physical form – some for health reasons, as in breast reductions and bariatric surgeries, others motivated by aesthetics or aspirations to western ideals of beauty, with nose, ear and eye jobs, breast enlargements and cosmetic face/neck surgery, desperate to reduce their shame and boost their confidence. Others, trapped inside a male or female form that feels alien to who they truly are, seek gender reassignment surgeries as they can't see any other way to live.

I've worked with a number of young people – male and female – who felt out of synch with their bodies. Actually, to say 'out of synch' is to underplay the feelings drastically: from my experience it begins with feelings of being different and not fitting in, then moves to discomfort with the physical form, before morphing into a desperation to change physically that is difficult to understand, even as a therapist. I've seen teenaged females endure the daily pain of strapping down their growing breasts; males with sprouting hair and genitalia they begin to despise – and the significant hit all this has on their mental health.

When these young people reflect, they will often tell you that their early attempts to voice their discomfort with their bodies or gender were brushed aside or ignored, so they learned silence as a coping, and later safety, mechanism. *If you disappear, you cannot be targeted – or ridiculed.* This is not always the fault of parents and the other adults in their worlds: we have to understand the extent to which societal norms shape thinking and behaviour.

Gender journeys are frequently as arduous for families as they are for those going through them. Some families, and more as society grows more accepting, are able to support their children, parents and partners through the change; but it is still hugely challenging and their loss of the person they thought they knew, and the future they thought they had with them, needs to be acknowledged too.

**

There's no blueprint for happiness in the wake of any form of surgical change. Psychologists see people do well after surgery – others struggle for years and some make no shift emotionally or mentally, despite radical physical change, which can surprise and disappoint them.

I understand the drive to change; our bodies walk in the world the way our minds don't, and tell a story about us in a way our minds can't – unless we force people to listen to the contents of them. So there is no shame in wanting to make the best of what we have; there's no shame in wanting to be true to ourselves or correct things that are holding us back from participating fully in life.

But we're playing a dangerous game when our efforts to change how we look destroy our health and threaten our safety. And we're being naive if we believe changing our physical appearance will change who we are.

Body Whispering

When life is Busy as F*ck, our bodies can become vessels for stress; our worries and fears can show up in aches and pains – in fact, this is often the only thing that makes us take it seriously. In that way, the physiological symptoms of stress can be useful: we'll go to the GP for heart palpitations, strange rashes and allergies, chest pain, headaches, a sore back or nagging stomach problems. But racing thoughts? Rumination? A feeling of overwhelm? Forget it. I need to save my doctors' visits for a Real Problem.

Except that stress is a Real Problem.

Stress plays out in our bodies more often than we want to acknowledge. Numerous studies have linked stress with illness including heart disease, increased blood pressure, gastrointestinal issues, immune deficiencies and weight problems. Tenuous links with various cancers remain hard to prove but I don't take much convincing: our bodies hold onto old wounds, memories and trauma, so it makes sense we will find some place to store them.

Our bodies whisper to us, they tell us what's wrong. That's why psychologists always ask people if they have any unexplained muscle aches and pains as part of a general assessment. Frequently the answer is yes, but they're not sure why. Or they suffer more than others seem to from colds and flu; they're exhausted and rundown and there's no clear reason for it – other than stress. Some people have been 'tested for everything' medically, with nothing conclusive found. They don't want to accept it could be an emotional problem, the legacy of their insanely stressed life – even when psychological assessment shows it to be true. It's hard on busy GPs, though, because people will rush through the door for a blood test or an X-ray, but they'll baulk at the suggestion they test for anxiety or depression.

Somatic problems – physical symptoms that can't be explained by a medical condition or physical cause – are set to grow exponentially as our stress levels continue to rise. Perhaps it's that when our minds can't tolerate any more stress our bodies catch the spillover. And why wouldn't the mind share the load with its closest ally? Especially if it means the host will pay attention to the immense stress they are under and do something about it.

I once saw a woman in her late 40s who reported neck and shoulder pain that had plagued her for years. She'd had every medical test going, but nothing showed up. It turned out her bipolar-disordered, alcoholic, difficult mother had loaded demands on her all her life – and was still doing it. As the 'good daughter' she had always done her best to keep her mother happy, but the resentment burned deep. One day she blurted out her mother had always been 'a massive pain in the neck'. Imagine her shock as she joined the dots. As she started to address this burden psychologically and put boundaries around her mother's unreasonable demands, the pain lifted. Interestingly, whenever her mother increased her phone contact and demands, the pain returned.

***

Stress can also show up in obsessions about our health. Health anxiety – formerly known as hypochondriasis – is a preoccupation with the belief one has, or is in danger of developing, a serious illness. People become obsessed with their bodies, monitoring their function and constantly scanning them for trouble. Normal bodily sensations can be misinterpreted as dangerous; tiny blips or abnormalities can bloom into debilitating fear.

I recall one woman telling me she had cancer. This would have been a shock, and I would have showed her all due empathy, if it had been her first revelation of this. But in the six months we had worked together, this was her third bout of cancer. Possibly her fourth.

I wanted to smile, but I couldn't risk that – you never know. 'Confirmed?' I asked.

'Not yet,' she said, leaning forward on the couch. 'I have an appointment with my GP this afternoon.'

Her earlier cancer 'scares' had been unfounded, and this one would likely go the same way. But if you think this woman was unhinged, you'd be wrong. She was smart, had a great job, a close family and was a lovely, quick-witted person. But that didn't stop her from whipping into a frenzy at the first sign of trouble in her body – every lump, every cough, every red mark or rash, every bruise. It was always, in her mind, cancer.

She had a full-blown case of health anxiety; she knew it – trying to get it under control was the primary reason she had come to therapy. But although she fully understood what was going on, and how it played out for her, she struggled to dampen it.

It's almost like when people carry their anxiety or stress in their bodies; it picks a vulnerable spot to show up in. Sometimes, as with this woman, it can be quickly traced to a specific event (her mother died of cancer at a young age) but the body can also hold onto general distress. That's why unexplained aches and pains often disappear when people get into a better space in their lives.

With any illness – mental or physical – it is critical to consider the person holistically, to look beyond a set of symptoms, to seek the likely origin of the problem and identify what might be maintaining it – because sometimes the key lies in the gains the person might be getting from being unwell. Love? Attention? Some downtime? Relief from the constant demands? If you are getting those things there's a very good reason to remain sick, so we have to build the case for the other side. You also have to draw out the unique strengths the person has to counter it.

Eat, Weigh, Love

Ask people what they don't like about their bodies and by far the most common answer is 'my weight'. The logic generally goes like this: 'If I could just drop 10 kg, get rid of this spare tyre, reduce a dress or pants size, my life would be fantastic'. Then they'll lay into themselves for their poor, or sabotaging, eating habits – and the exercise they don't take or have stopped taking in the crazy rush of life.

Even when people haven't sought help specifically for weight issues, it will often creep into the conversation. Or their angst over their weight, and themselves for being unable to reduce it, will underpin other difficulties, such as depression or social and health anxieties. Some people will blurt out their frustration on the first meeting; others will avoid the topic, taking you in a circular and often interesting, funny route through their lives before getting to the source of their pain.

As one woman once told me, 'I hope you realise I am purposely entertaining you so I won't have to talk about my weight.'

I did. But she told a great story, and it was her session, so I let it go.

And another witty woman after several sessions: 'I love talking about my weight. It's way more fun than having to do anything about it.'

I enjoyed her tales; she was hilarious. It was better value than a ticket to the comedy festival. But my guilt at not making any progress on her behalf weighed heavily on me. I shouldn't have worried. When she finished trawling her history and telling stories, she discharged herself. 'You've given me plenty to think about. I'll be back when I'm ready to do something.'

I never saw her again.

When Our Eating Messes Us Up

Eating disorders are most commonly linked with being underweight – but that's misleading.

Disordered or problematic eating can't be pegged to a particular body type. It shows up in all sorts of forms, shapes and bodies – overweight, underweight, everything in between – and in legions of people of average weight who go about their business with their minds held to ransom by food, every meal a minefield of confusion and decision-making.

What you can't see, you can't know. Just as people are experts in hiding their struggles from the world, so it is with food and weight. Maybe it's especially so with food and weight, because of the shame and fear that often goes with it. Like the woman sitting next to you at work who is counting down the minutes until she is allowed the third of the six meals she has carefully planned for the day. Or the slim young dad in the park with his kids plotting to tell his worried wife he has already eaten when she gets home so he can skip another meal. Or the gym junkie who broke her own heart when she dumped her lovely boyfriend because she could not bear to eat dinner with him. Or the student who can't go to a restaurant with friends without downloading the menu and spending three days agonising over what he can safely eat. Or the lonely man who orders pizzas at midnight to maintain the weight he is scared to lose because being big is the only way he knows of being loved.

***

Anyone who has worked in the eating disorder field will tell you these problems don't fit neatly into the classifications offered by the manuals of psychiatric disorder. People don't starve, binge, fast, restrict, run two hours a day, eat only broccoli for breakfast, avoid eating with others or in restaurants, or spend hours planning their food intake, according to classified lists. They make up their own combinations, responses or ways of coping in the world.

Orthorexia nervosa – the obsession with healthy or clean eating – is the big (and silent) mover and shaker in eating disorders. That's because it's 'acceptable', even lauded, to say you want to eat healthily – after all, that's the message we're all pushing to ourselves, our families and our kids. But 'healthy eating' (or even obsessions with the likes of gluten, dairy-free, vegetarian, paleo and vegan diets) can be a mask for controlling food behaviour that glides unseen under the radar. I've seen a number of people who've told me they had medical conditions that demanded they Eat Healthy At All Costs. Their GP/specialist has said so. Often this means they are hiding some disordered eating behaviour but unless their weight reflects it, it's impossible to be sure. And, unless they are dangerously unwell, you can't push someone to change it. Interestingly, male eating disorders often present in this guise: 'I can't eat vegetables or meat or bread due to a particular medical condition' – but it's always underpinned by marked anxiety. Possibly it's because the stigma of eating disorder is even bigger for males: it's okay to drastically curb your eating for a physical cause, but if it's all in your head? Maybe not.

Anorexia nervosa, or any derivative problem associated with extreme weight loss, gets the most attention because it scares people: it carries the very real prospect that someone might die. But I've always found that emphasis on the underweight undermines the equally real struggles of the extremely overweight. They could die too – but we don't panic about that.

While we worry about dangerously thin people, we scorn those who 'can't stop eating'. While we say the seriously thin 'can't help' their weight issues, we mock those who we think can. How is that fair? And, unless we struggle with these things personally, how would we know?

Eating difficulties, in all their variations, are difficult to pin down because cause is due to a constellation of factors. Sometimes the roots lie in a chaotic or neglectful early environment, sometimes not – so it's important not to rush into pointing the finger at family dysfunction. Sometimes trauma can be a catalyst, particularly in overweight issues.

In underweight disorders, research has shown links with trauma, loss, control, perfectionism, seeking approval/love or protection, wanting to excel and identity issues. Triggers can range from family pressure, a social media post, light teasing or hurtful bullying, a critical remark by a coach or teacher, right through to a sudden self-consciousness of physical maturation, particularly in the case of girls. *I'm bigger than all the other girls. I have hips and breasts and they don't.* Perhaps the biggest difficulty with eating disorders lies in the vice-like grip they take, often quickly. They snake through minds and personalities, often leading parents and families to say things like they 'don't recognise' their loved one; 'this thing has changed them.'

It's been claimed that anorexia nervosa is a soul sickness. I don't like or agree with that because it sounds like you need some sort of exorcism to get to the other side. You don't. Anorexia is a disease or disorder, not a genetic implant; and there is always a significant thread of anxiety running through it. But to have a shot at recovery, you do need a client who wants to be helped – and that can be the trickiest part.

Extremely underweight clients, even those who willingly come to treatment, face a terrible dilemma. They want to get better but they don't want what that will mean – weight gain. So they won't engage, or they'll do it superficially, or they'll pretend and think you can't see through it. They'll lie, they'll charm, they'll trick, and they'll tell their mother they hate her and they never want to come back.

They'll keep you tiptoeing across eggshells, along with everyone else on their care team, because of the threat of death. Because mortality rates are the highest of the psychiatric disorders (5–6% for anorexia nervosa) and cure rates somewhat masked, the focus has to stay on physical health and safety, which is the antithesis of the best way to treat these conditions.

The best way is not to talk about food or eating or weight. But that's not always easy. Or possible.

A young woman who'd been diagnosed with anorexia nervosa was booked in for an appointment by her frantic mother. Her skin was almost blue, she was whippet thin and looked several years younger than her 16 years. She had refused to go to her GP but said she would see me, a psychologist, perhaps hoping for a lighter hand. She wouldn't let her mother leave the room.

I was new to the work then and half way through the first session waded in with the need to weigh herself on an agreed basis. You don't understand the terror associated with such a request until the first time you hand it out. The sweet face that had been presented to me, and delighted in talking about school and her interests, flashed a dark shadow.

'Why do I need to do that? Why don't you trust me to do what you say?'

Weighing was in the interests of her safety – and it was necessary according to my code of ethics – but I should have taken my time and locked in the relationship before I went there. I should have – but I was freaked out by my own need for safety. *What if she died on my watch?*

So I insisted and I blew it. I knew her mother would never get her back to a second appointment. And I was right.

So What to Do in a Busy as F*ck World?

We can talk all we like about being healthy but it can take us around a track with no end. When we're rushed and stressed we tend to drop our healthy habits and do things that make us feel worse: grab a takeaway or chocolate bar on the run, stop going to the gym, binge eat then skip meals to compensate, spend way too many evenings on the sofa with reality TV and a glass of wine (more than one, usually).

All of that makes us panic we're on a slippery slope to nowhere good and if our weight continues to tick up at its current rate … well, where will it end? But panicking doesn't take us anywhere. When people genuinely want to lead healthier lives, they need some practical solutions to help.

Here are three of my most popular strategies: (1) how to change your dysfunctional relationship with food; (2) how to exercise when you can't stand it; and (3) advice for parents, especially mothers, who want to promote healthy body images in their kids.

1. Changing Your Relationship with Food

'I've been in an abusive relationship for 20 years,' a young woman once told me by way of introduction.

Given that she looked barely 30, her revelation startled me. I braced myself for a hardcore story of abuse, violent or sexual, a threat not just to her wellbeing but her safety.

'It's controlling me – day and night,' she said. 'I can't think of anything else. I need it to stop. I need to get out. But I'm trapped; I just can't leave.'

She smiled then, and I understood her metaphor: her abusive partner was food. They had 'met' when she was 11. She'd matured early, begun menstruating, was bigger than most of her friends, and been whipped off to Weight Watchers by her slim and well-meaning mother. Her mother who, of all the things in all the world, did not want to be the mother of a *fat kid*.

This young woman was typical of many who seek psychological help for struggles with food, weight and their bodies. She didn't like her body but, more than that, she was tired of the relentless battle in her head. She wanted to be free of it, to find a way to move forward.

The psychological consequences of being overweight or obese can include a raft of issues that people often keep hidden, or don't acknowledge, for far too long.

Being overweight might not cause or trigger depression but 'hating' your physical self can maintain depression, anxiety, undermine confidence and self-worth, which can spill over into the rest of your life, impacting relationships, families and opportunities.

Many overweight people report low mood and motivation, irritability, exhaustion, various forms of anxiety, loss of pleasure in activities, social withdrawal, guilt and shame. People will say they feel 'flat, stuck and defeated' and struggle to form a hopeful view of the future.

Changing Your Food Relationship

But how? you ask. How do I break it off? How do I end my exhausting, addictive, dysfunctional relationship with food? Is there a way to train my brain to relax?

The truthful answer is you can't change your weight permanently without understanding your food psychology: your biology and family/cultural history, people, triggers and hotspots, strengths and the way you interact with food.

You can diet and exercise all you like – and that can work – but, without greater knowledge of the way you operate and some authentic incentive, it won't last.

So here are the key steps you need to follow to make permanent change:

- Have a *real, specific, lasting* reason for losing weight.
  Make sure it is yours and not something someone else
  thinks would work for you. Write it down and look at it
  frequently. This reason should be significant enough to
  help you correct your behaviour if you fall off the wagon.

- Change your *behaviour.*
  Be honest about what you eat. Reducing your food
  intake/eating differently and increasing your activity will
  help kickstart new thinking. Psychologically, the best way
  to break a bad habit is to replace it with something else.
  So do something different. Start small but start today.

- Clean up your food *environment*.
  Remove temptations wherever possible (such as in your home) and don't expose yourself unnecessarily to food 'traps' like work morning teas or people who always eat unhealthily. Healthy food decisions are much easier to make when your environment supports them.

- Challenge your *thoughts* and *beliefs* around food.
  First you need to identify those (often from your past) that are holding you back. What are your vulnerabilities and weaknesses and how can you address them? What new thought could you replace your old thinking with? Example: (Old thought) I need to eat everything on my plate. (Replacement thought) It's fine to eat only what I like and to leave some food behind.

- Reduce your *stress* levels.
  When we're stressed we often seek comfort or fulfilment in food, which plays havoc with the best weight loss intentions. Identify the biggest stress in your life and do something about it – even if it's just something small.

- Work on *yourself*, not your weight.
  View yourself as a person, prioritise that person and treat him/her well. Self-care is your overall goal; eating well is a subset of that.

Above all, be realistic. As the saying goes, good things take time. Stop focusing on your body and make your mind do some work too. After all, you are a person with a bum attached – not the other way around.

2. How to Exercise When You Can't Stand It

A quick guide to doing it and not giving up

'I wish I loved to exercise,' the woman said. 'Then I might do some.'

The woman was typical of many who struggle with their weight – and despair at sustaining any form of physical activity. She'd tried all the usual things: gym, classes, yoga, Pilates, dance forms, personal training, weights, hill walks. She'd tried social groups, motivational music and podcasts. Nothing would stick.

So she'd assumed her deeply embedded distaste for all things physical, except sex, was driving it. *And* she assumed people who do exercise regularly are having the time of their lives.

Wrong. Regular exercisers come in all shapes, sizes and motivations. Only a few are riding a heady wave of endorphins. You can tell who they are because they're posting deltoid-flexing selfies on social media.

Most of us don't want to be seen alive, or even dead, in activewear. Most of us are dragging our reluctant butts into the fray, secretly praying for an invitation to any boring thing so we can get out of it.

So we're all in good company.

Loving exercise is not the key. They key is to love that you can (still) move your body. It's to love that you've done it – after it's over. It's to love that you are making an effort for your health and longevity. It's to love that you have not given up on yourself.

So here's a quick guide to kicking off an exercise habit that will go the distance:

* **Lock the pantry, seal the fridge.** There's a bigger player than physical activity here – food. If weight loss is your goal don't expect exercise to do all the heavy lifting. Sort out your food intake to go with it, otherwise you'll just be setting up a weird compensation scheme: if I do *that*, I can eat *that*.

* **Write the end of the story first.** Write down why you want to set up an exercise habit for life. If it's a short-term reason only, you're in trouble. What happens when the wedding's over? What happens when you hit your goal weight? It has to be something meaningful to you over time – otherwise it won't last.

* **Leave your past behind you.** It can help to know the historical reason for why we're stuck but it can also turn into an excuse – and if you dwell on it, you're gone. Once you know why you want to exercise regularly, bring yourself into the present. Think right here, right now.

* **The best way to ditch a (bad) habit is to replace it.** You've just read this in the section about changing your food relationship. But I'm okay with being repetitive when I know something works. Figure out a new, achievable exercise routine. Think about whether it's doable – not whether it's enjoyable.

* **Undercook it.** Whatever you've planned, cut it in half. I will go to the gym five days a week for life (from a standing start of nothing) won't work. Choose something you'll be able to keep up – or return to when you fall over (because you will). Three times a week is ideal.

* **Use a visual cue.** Put your walking shoes, with their bright orange laces, by the door. Hopefully they will speak to you when you walk past.

* **Block your feelings.** Not generally advocated by psychologists but we need an exception here: barring illness, *never* ask yourself how you feel about exercising. The answer will never be 'Woohoo. Bring it on.' Just pull on your shoes and go do it.

* **Give yourself a gold star.** *Always* tag a reward to your routine. Time for coffee, reading a magazine or blog, something you like to do. You've earned it. Beware food rewards, though – or you might just have another habit you need to break.

3. My Teen Is Eating Weirdly – What Do I Do?

This is by far the most common question parents (especially mothers) ask about their children's eating (especially daughters), because they want to be able to pass on the right messages.

Q. My 14-year-old daughter has begun to eat strangely. She says she's not hungry at dinner time; she pushes food around her plate. I think she's lost a little weight and she's showing a sudden interest in joining a gym. Is this normal for her age group? Should I be worried?

In eating difficulties, early intervention does predict the best outcomes so it's smart to be in tune with any changes to your teen's habits, eating or otherwise.

Mothers tend to be on high alert for underweight eating disorders, due to the negative publicity of such cases, media messages that value 'thin' and shame 'fat' and our own insecurities around food and our bodies. Many of us know all too well the dark places this obsessional thinking can take us. We *do not* want our daughters lurching from diet to diet or to inherit our hang-ups.

And that can make us hyper-vigilant to any changes in eating behaviour – even those that are a normal part of growing up and becoming independent.

Here are the key early warning signs, followed by some tips for building a healthy body image. Note that I'm talking about girls because they are by far the biggest concern for parents:

Early warning signs may include:

- An exaggerated preoccupation with body or food.
- Sudden changes in eating behaviours (e.g. deliberately skipping meals, not wanting to eat with the family, immediately heading to the bathroom after meals).
- Increase in checking behaviours (weighing, measurement, looking in the mirror).
- Eating/exercise begins to impact involvement in other normally enjoyed activities or relationships.
- Eating/exercise is prioritised over everything else.
- Social withdrawal (could have other causes such as depression, drugs).
- Intermittent or ceased menstruation (when it has previously been regular).

Building a healthy body image

Obviously, prevention is the best 'cure', but parents can't control all the influences in their teen's world, and must not blame themselves when a child begins to show signs of disordered eating.

Here are some tips for developing and fostering a healthy body image. Again, this relates primarily to girls, although some points are relevant across genders:

- Lead by example. Model healthy behaviour to children (especially daughters) and watch the way you speak about eating, exercise and your own body. Try not to eat 'differently' or 'separately' from the family. Your teen will absorb what she sees and hears.
- Explain body changes during puberty. Explain that weight gain is a normal part of development and maturation.
- Talk about media messages. Counter messages that only a certain body type is acceptable and that being 'hot'

or 'skinny' is most important. Notice what your teen is reading or watching and encourage them to discuss and question.

- Monitor internet use. Check out your teen's use of social networking sites, particularly around body image. Talk about what they are posting and viewing.
- Discuss self-image. Provide reassurance that healthy body shapes vary. Ask your teen what she likes about herself and say what you like about her too. Your acceptance helps build self-esteem and resilience.
- Use positive language. Speak about food and exercise in positive ways. Discourage family and friends from using hurtful nicknames and joking about people who are overweight.
- Establish healthy eating and physical activity habits. Help build knowledge about healthy food types and quantities.
- Talk up strengths. Help her discover what she's good at; expose her to women who are famous for their achievements, rather than their looks.
- Praise achievements. Value what she does, rather than what she looks like. Look for opportunities to praise effort, skill, personality and achievements.
- Encourage positive friendships. Friends who accept your teen for who she is can be a healthy influence.

Finally, remember that many teenagers exhibit these kinds of symptoms – it doesn't mean you are on your way to a full-blown eating disorder. If you are worried, seek professional advice and/ or an assessment. Putting your hand up early gives you the best chance of a good outcome.

What to Do When It All Goes Wrong

'My husband's been screwing another woman twice a week,' Meghan says. It's one of the one best opening lines I've ever heard.

She's in her forties and looks like a highly stressed working mother of three, which, I later find out, is exactly what she is. She's also had no sleep for days, since the discovery of her husband's affair.

'How do you know it's twice a week?'

The minute I say this I know I have failed the empathy test by focusing on the wrong thing, but the words are out before I can clamp my lips over them. She looks at me with a new respect.

'He goes to the gym on Tuesday and Thursday nights and his sports kit never needs washing. I don't know … a woman would never be that stupid.'

We both laugh, but it has a hollow ring because we both understand the potential implications of her husband's cheating, Meghan because she has been thinking of nothing else for the past fortnight, me because I've heard similar versions of this story many times before.

Meghan backs up and tells me her story, the words pouring out in a torrent. She and Anthony had met at university and were *that* couple, Megs and Ant, the envy of all their friends because they'd found each other so young. They'd married in their early 20s but waited almost a decade before having their kids, who were now aged 10, eight and five. She had recently returned to work and was finding it hard to juggle, to keep everyone happy.

She said she thought they had a forever marriage. 'It wasn't perfect; life's full-on with work and three kids. But I thought we were good, better than most other couples I know. I'd do anything for Ant and he knows it. I had no idea he wasn't happy with me ... or with us. He works long hours and he's always on his phone ... but so am I. If anything, I'm worse because I'm involved in so much with the kids and everything. A few months ago he joined the gym at his work. He said he wanted to lose the bit of weight he'd put on in the past year. He decided Tuesday and Thursdays were his workout nights. Ha!'

'When I finally worked up the courage to ask him about it, he didn't even bother to deny it. He just said, "Yes, there's someone else ... a woman I met at work." He said it wasn't serious, she'd initiated it, and he'd end it.'

'Has he done that – ended it? Is he sorry?' I asked, because the intent of both parties is critical to outcomes. Remorse is a key indicator of whether the relationship can be restored – even then it can be a long way back.

'That's just it. I don't think it's over. He's still always on his phone and making excuses to go out some nights. I can't sleep, I'm spinning things around and around in my head. Who is she? How old is she? How long has this been happening? Where? Why? What was wrong with us? With me?'

With that, the energy suddenly left her body; exhaustion washed over her face. 'I'm absolutely shattered. I haven't told anyone, not even my sister, I'm too ashamed. Nothing like this has ever happened to me – I've always been the good girl, the one who did the right thing, kept everyone happy.'

Then she paused, whispering. 'I'm just so worried. We have a big mortgage, three kids and Ant earns a lot more than me. What if he loves this woman. What if we're over? What am I going to do?'

***

How do I cope? is perhaps the most frequently asked question in psychology. It comes in many different packages but the fallout is often the same: anxiety ramping up in the face of uncertainty.

Meghan described herself as a People Pleaser, someone who would do anything for anyone. This could make her particularly vulnerable as she might frame Ant's cheating as the ultimate rejection of her bid for approval. Adding to her distress is the shock of her discovery, which has thrown her mental state into chaos. Relationship breakdowns, or fractures, are never quickly resolved, so she faces a prolonged period of uncertainty and fear.

Change comes at us in myriad ways. Sometimes it is creeping change we've spotted but feel powerless to stop; other times it bursts through like a freight train, barely giving us time to leap out of the way. Either way, when we are already Busy as F*ck, it can be an exercise in survival, before we even get to thinking and functioning effectively.

Psychologists need to avoid handing out the sort of tired old advice that dominates the internet: work through a grief model; put your negative thoughts on a leaf and float them down the river and on the other side of all this you will be a greater, grander person full of higher learnings.

No-one wants to hear that when they're in shock. Meghan probably would have slapped me if I'd gone there.

Crap happens. At some point in our lives we are all tested. While we shouldn't walk around waiting for the sky to fall in, we need to understand that no-one leads a life free of difficulty, so it's important that we arm ourselves to cope when it lands.

Difficulties can show up in any segment of the pizza: relationships, work, money, families and health. It can be something someone has done to us, something beyond our control or something we've done wrong ourselves, leading to shame, guilt and a long trail of remorse.

In summary, there are three ways things can go all wrong:

1. **Shock.** Out-of-the-blue events, leading to a swift and devastating change in our circumstances, such as Meghan's discovery of her partner's cheating, loss of a job, the diagnosis of serious illness or death of a loved one.
2. **Slow burner.** It could be a deteriorating relationship, a partner's alcoholism, financial problems, a chronic health condition, difficulties with children or parents or even hating a job you can't leave. Stress slowly builds, having an ongoing impact on physical and emotional health, relationships and everything else in our lives.
3. **Super-combo.** This is when you're already on a slow-burner then you plunge into crisis. This can be extremely taxing because mind and body are already stretched to maximum and the extra loading can take people to breaking point.

How we deal with difficulty, and associated change, is often dictated by our core resilience but it's hard to predict accurately someone's reaction unless they've been there before – and even then, people can react differently. When people are thrown into crisis, like Meghan was, the most helpful thing is to put some practical coping strategies in place. Meghan will probably want and need to unpack the meaning of all this later on, but for now she needs to cope with all she has on her already overloaded plate – and in her mind.

So here is a quick guide to what to do when trouble strikes:

Seven First Steps to Coping with Crap

* Shut the front door (and the back door too).

You need time to yourself to grasp what has happened. Shock and raw emotion throw us – and a common early reaction is to deny or avoid thinking about what has happened. This can lead us to shut down, to go into 'helpless' or victim mode when we have things we need to do. The quicker we can acknowledge (we don't have to yet accept) the truth, the sooner we can begin to shuffle forward. But don't isolate yourself for too long – that will make things worse.

* Cry or get mad.

You're allowed to feel pain, express feelings and show vulnerability. It's normal and healthy. If you're not the tearful type at least allow yourself to identify and name what you are feeling: sadness, rage, fear, devastation – or murderous thoughts of revenge. (Just don't act on them.)

* Stop crying or getting mad.

Being able to regulate your emotions is equally important, especially if you have others, such as children, relying on you. Tears are good, but don't let yourself drown in them. Your emotions will swing, clash and change – that's okay but beware of letting them stop you from doing what you need to do. So set boundaries around your emotions if you can and distract yourself with other activities.

* Name your people.

Write down two lists. (1) The people you need to look after and (2) those you can fully trust to support you. This will help you organise your thinking and priorities – and know when to say 'yes' and 'no' – when your head is full and the tasks are piling up.

* Do a daily high five.

Focus on what you *can* do. Make a list of *five things* you need to do now, or quickly. Then move to a daily list, which you should write for yourself every evening so you know where to start when you wake up in the morning. Your daily list should not contain more than five items or you'll feel overwhelmed. Then pick the most important thing on the list and tackle it methodically.

* Some things (should) remain the same.

When large-scale change occurs, or is ongoing, it can seem like your whole world has been thrown into turmoil. But not everything needs to change. It's super important to keep ordinary life routines going. So if the problem is at work, keep things tracking on the outside and at home (your fitness, your eating, your relationship). This is particularly important for kids when faced with change as in a separation or divorce; the stability provided by routines: activities – school and friendships – promotes better coping and outcomes.

* Breathe.

Psychologists are boringly repetitive with this instruction but we figure centuries of evidence can't be wrong. Don't gulp at the air because it will wind you up and may cause you to hyperventilate. Slow, even breathing gives you a chance to chill out, centre yourself, feel more anchored. And that means you'll be able to think rationally about what you need to do. You'll find some breathing exercises later in this section.

* Say yes to the fish pie (even if you don't like fish pie).
Ask for (or least accept) offers of support. Friends, family and colleagues are often willing but don't know what to say or do. You will help yourself – as well as them – by asking for what you need, even a meal or something tiny, or at least allowing them to be there for you.

***

Now What?

In the early stages of shock or change, it is often a matter of survival; of doing what you need to do to look after yourself and anyone in your care. In some ways, despite the shock, it can be easier because you have so much to do in a practical sense. But when all that subsides, the mental ghosts can come out to play. If and when they do, here are three more things worth knowing:

* You don't have to get to the other side to be okay.
Often we aim for 'all this' to be over. That's not always smart because it can take a long time for things to settle or improve. If you've lost a loved one, for example, that is something you learn to live alongside, rather than to 'move on' from. It's better to focus on what you can, and need to, do right now. Even on a bad day it is possible for something – however tiny – good to happen. Your job is to look for it, notice it and absorb it.

* Your best resources are inside you.
No matter what happens you have the same resources inside you. The same character. The same strengths. When things are

uncertain it is easy to lose sight of those. But you are who you were. Use the best of yourself to help.

* Be a different person.

Not better, just different. This one comes last for a reason. While some change is horrific it can force us to develop parts of ourselves we didn't know existed. You don't have to think about this when you are struggling – but keep it in mind for later. Change may ultimately be used for the greater good.

Resilience: Being Tough for Life

Resilience, also known as mental toughness or grit, is the hottest commodity in psychology because everyone wants to know how to survive the chaos. Employers want strategies for staff, parents want tools for kids; all of us want fortitude for ourselves. But whenever I mention resilience to people I work with, their eyes glaze over. We all know it's worthy but something about that word makes people feel tired and bored, even me, who loves this stuff.

The best definition of resilience I've heard came from Grace, a 16-year-old who had white scars right up both thighs from where she'd slashed at them with a razor blade. She showed me a picture of a skeleton and told me that was what she wanted to look like, it was her ideal body – a collection of bones.

Grace's worried mother had sent her along to work on her resilience, to get some tools for coping. People have different ideas about what resilience means so I asked Grace how she saw it.

She said she'd come back to me on that and we spent the rest of the session talking about death. At the end of the hour she told me she had the answer to my question. I was so caught up in her story I could barely remember what the question was.

'Kia Kaha,' Grace said. 'That's what resilience is.'
'Kia Kaha
I roto i to Whakaaro, I roto i to Tinana. I roto i to Ngakau'
Stand strong
In your mind, in your body, in your heart.

(translation from te reo Māori,
the native language of New Zealand)

I loved her framing of resilience: it's real, it does not confine psychology solely to its traditional home – the head – and it came to me from a young woman who knew better than me what it was like to be down in the emotional trenches. It's the definition I've used ever since.

Standing strong (in your mind, body and heart) is so important, as how we withstand and eventually rise from our difficulties, from everything life throws at us, is ultimately the measure of us.

How to Build a 'Hot' Mind

Many people still prefer the term 'mental toughness' to resilience, particularly in the world of sports.

Mental toughness has a hard, untouchable aura, sort of like Navy SEALs, who hold their breath under water for minutes at a time, drag military dummies through mud and leap through blazing rings of fire.

But to hold fast to a military theme doesn't work for most people because we don't tend to aspire to that kind of toughness. I don't know about you but I don't have much incentive for dragging military dummies through mud on my weekends – I'd rather read a book.

The point is, though, being mentally tough is critical. Not just to survive the darts and daggers life throws at us but also to give us the spark to dig out of ruts, change direction, to be bold in our choices.

A young man I worked with gave me a different way of looking at it. He was struggling with anxiety, feeling out of his depth in a new job and had recently broken up with his first serious girlfriend, which had sent his mind into overdrive. When I asked him what he wanted from our work he was clear.

'I want to build a hot mind.'

'What do you mean?'

'I want my mind to be clear and calm and strong. I want a mind that can handle stress, that doesn't overthink everything, that can deal with ... life.'

It was a useful analogy. People relate to the idea of building mental muscle, of working out mentally, of developing mental skills that will make them fit and strong for life.

A 'hot' or well-trained mind helps us to:

- Cope with stress and adversity. Light the way back from tough times. Wash clean our emotional wounds so they don't infect us for the rest of our lives.
- Thrive in the world. Give us courage. Open us up to growth, change and possibility.

Can You Build a 'Hot' Mind?

Some people, for genetic, character and environmental reasons, are mentally stronger than others. Sometimes, though, it's because they have had easier lives; they haven't been as harshly tested.

The great news is that you can *build* mental strength, you can take what you've got and make it better. But – like anything in psychology – you need to start from where you are, and that begins with an honest assessment.

Test your mental strength with this quiz. Answer with 'mostly', 'sometimes' or 'not often'.

1. In a crisis I can remain calm and focus on taking useful actions for myself and loved ones.
2. I am generally optimistic. When tough times strike I believe it's temporary and that I will be able to overcome it.
3. I adapt quickly to new situations and/or to change of any kind.
4. I am able to find (appropriate) humour in most situations and I am able to laugh at myself.
5. I can handle uncertainty; I don't need to know for sure what is happening to calm myself down.
6. When stressed I have at least one reliable way of calming myself down (other than exercise, medication or drugs).
7. I have people in my life I can rely on and I'm not afraid to ask them for help.
8. I have a healthy view of myself (I'd rate my self-esteem 7/10 or higher).
9. I am bold in my choices when I need to make change.

Results

If you answered 'mostly' to most or all of the questions, great. You are emotionally robust and in a position to help and support others. Do what you need to do to stay there.

If you answered 'sometimes' to most or all of the questions, you are doing okay but you should definitely invest time in building your mental muscle.

If you answered 'not often', take notice. There's work to be done: growing your self-understanding and having a good awareness of your strengths will immeasurably improve your life.

Start Where You Are

Research indicates the number one quality we need for resilience is *adaptability*, to be able to think flexibly and to adjust quickly to change when necessary.

So start there. Check your answers to 3) and 5) and 9) and if they are not what you'd like – or need – them to be, identify a time where you backed off from a challenge or were negative about it. Ask yourself what you could have done differently. Then the next time you are challenged or need to take a chance, flex your mental muscle. Step forward, not back: it'll make all the difference.

Get the Mental Edge

Beyond the general whirl of life, mental toughness is a key ingredient in exceptional performance. We've all heard of the 'top two inches', that invisible extra one to five per cent. Mentally tough people are able to manage their minds through adversity, failure, pain and extreme pressure to perform at their peak. They are in charge of their mental state (as much as anyone can be), which promotes best results.

Mental toughness is founded on unique combinations we can't see or easily measure: biology, history, experience, insight, learning and tools – so, on top of our natural resources, there's a lot we can learn. But here's a secret: *Mental toughness is as much about what you don't do – as what you do. Exceptional performers are able to bounce between them.*

So here are some things to think about:

Five Things Mentally Tough People Don't Do

* Think in black and white.

Black and white or rigid thinking will make you overly judgmental and keep you stuck. Flexible thinking is the hallmark of resilience. People who can adapt quickly can be counted on to cope best in any situation. The world is not black and white; there are an awful lot of grey areas. So Think Grey: introduce some shadow into your thinking – it'll make you bolder and tougher when adversity strikes.

* Chase certainty to calm down.

Life is uncertain. Change is inevitable. Sometimes we need to change – we *have* to change – in order to cope with difficulty and to grow. So learning to live with uncertainty is a better, healthier aim than trying to control the world around us. Tell yourself it is okay not to know the outcome, then immerse yourself in doing what you need to do right here, right now.

* Let their feelings rule.

Mentally tough people are not devoid of emotions – they are able to express and manage their emotions, and be vulnerable when necessary. But they don't allow distressful or negative feelings to swamp them to the point of inaction. They don't allow their feelings to push them into doing things they regret. Whatever happens, they are able to think rationally, then act clearly and decisively – no matter what their feelings are doing.

* Globalise their fears.

When you're scared or worried it's easy to let your fear of the situation spill into a much larger 'global' deal. For example, I've been dumped so I will always be alone and lonely. I can't get a job so I'm destined to be unemployed and broke. When mentally tough people feel afraid, they are able to attach their fear to the specific event or circumstance. This partner cheated on me so that partner was no good for me. I missed out on this job for this reason; there are other jobs that will suit me better. Hooking fears to specifics makes difficulties seem smaller and therefore much easier to cope with.

* Home in on what went badly.

When things go wrong, it's easy to zero in on your flaws and mistakes, which then cause you to beat up on yourself. Mentally tough people don't allow failures or setbacks to dominate their thinking and bring them down. They acknowledge what went wrong and work out ways to counter it without losing sight of their strengths. They are able to see what went right, too, and build on that.

* Ignore their wins.

People often don't know how mentally tough they are until adversity strikes. Why not start now? Every time you deal with a difficult situation or rise from a setback, acknowledge it, think about how you did it and bank it. Then it's yours to draw on any time you like.

***

Before You Fall Down the Rabbit Hole, Do This

Psychologists feel a beat of hope when someone says they want to do more to look after themselves. Self-care is the first step in digging yourself out of whatever deep, dark hole you've fallen into.

But if we were up for lecturing people (which we're not because it doesn't work) we'd say self-care should start before a crisis. We'd push for people to give their minds as much care and attention as they do their bodies, which get rushed to the doctor or the physiotherapist or rested and plied with ice whenever anything goes wrong.

We'd want everyone to prioritise their mental health and fitness.

But we're biased, naturally.

Obviously, there's no one-size-fits-all self-care strategy because people have different operating systems, strengths and interests. But here are two strategies that, if used well and regularly, can serve us all:

1. The self-care checklist
2. Meditation for the slightly suspicious

The Self-Care Checklist

When life gets busy we struggle to take care of ourselves. Our healthy habits, along with our good intentions, take a hike and so we get the double whammy: stress combined with a lack of self-care.

So down the rabbit hole we go – and that rabbit hole is a densely populated place. There is a lot we can do to prevent going there, or at least make the burrow more cosy. So hit up the checklist below to make sure you have the basics covered.

* Eat, Sleep and Move

It'd be patronising to dwell on this one. These are the things your mother (hopefully) will have taught you. So eat well, get the rest your body requires and move your body – at the very least take it out for a walk. Look after the basics and the basics will look after you.

* Go Outside

Get into nature – research shows 'a walk in the wild' (or even the park) boosts mental health. Get some fresh air and sunlight whenever possible. And tap into the benefits of walking: not only is it good for your body, a rhythmic walk is a basic form of meditation (if it's without earplugs, audiobooks, podcasts, music). Try to notice your surroundings, describe them to yourself and, if necessary, count your steps to keep yourself in the moment. Repeat in chunks: e.g. count to 50 then begin again.

* Bookend your day (and why routines help)

Morning routines (beyond rolling out of bed, showering and eating) can be helpful to anchor and kickstart your day, particularly if you are feeling low and anxious. All the cool (and successful) people use them – or at least they say they do. While there is little scientific evidence for this, *routines are definitely helpful in the management of depression, pain and anxiety, when you want to reboot your life or when you want to 'get sh*t done'.* They provide the necessary structure to help us move forward or to hang good habits on.

Evening routines help you relax and promote good sleep hygiene and habits. But beware of making your routines so onerous that 1) they make you feel more stressed; and 2) you won't be able to stick to them. They should be something that you practice regularly and rely on.

* Something wonderful's going to happen.

Stake out things to look forward to. Have short-term (next weekend) and long-term (this year) events planned. It keeps you feeling excited – or at the very least with a reason to push forward when you're struggling.

* Breathe in. And out.

Show me how you breathe and I'll tell you who you are. Breathing is the simplest way to slow down and relax – it's portable too. Anxiety literature is awash with the benefits of diaphragmatic breathing. When you are stressed your breathing will be too rapid and too shallow. When you take a breath in, it should go all the way down through your body.

So here are two simple breathing exercises:

1. **5–10–20 Breathing.** Lie down, place your hands on your stomach. Take a deep breath in – if you are doing this correctly, your stomach should rise, not your chest. Breathe until you notice your hands rising with the in-breath.

   Take a deep breath as you slowly count to five, hold for a count of 10, breathe out for 20. It is the outward breath that most helps to release tension. Repeat the cycle five times, twice a day and/or whenever you feel tense. It can be difficult at first but persevere – it will give you some ownership over your anxiety.

2. **Don't-count-sheep breathing.** I don't know many people who've had success with the sheep-counting exercise. So try this instead; it's helpful for getting to sleep. Breathe steadily in and out. On the out breath, count backwards from 100 in threes (i.e. breathe in, breathe out, 100; breathe in, breathe out, 97; breathe in, breathe out, 94). It takes your busy brain away from those wild thoughts and gives it something to focus on but it's not too taxing. If you get all the way back to zero, start again. It does work!

* Relax your Muscles

Being able to calm down on the spot is a fantastic skill to be able to call on. You can use this to release tension wherever you are – sitting or standing. Moving from head to toe, tense and release each body part/muscle group. Hold the tension in the muscle for 10 seconds, then relax. If you are not somewhere you can do this physically, visualise yourself doing it, one muscle group at a time.

* Feel the Love

Connect. Smile. Nod. Touch (appropriately). Be in the world. Research shows social connection at all levels contributes to longevity and life satisfaction. When you are feeling isolated it's super important to connect – even via a text message or, better still, a phone call.

* Look Up and Out.

Raise your head from whatever you are doing occasionally. Talk a break. Go for a walk. Linger over lunch. Look at something beautiful. Or someone. Sit still. Have a laugh. Sing. Remind yourself that for all its chaos, and sometimes drudgery, your life still has much to offer you. And you to it.

Be Still Thy Wayward Mind: Meditation and Mindfulness

Meditation is the umbrella term for an ancient technique promoting mental relaxation and spiritual harmony. *Mindfulness* is a form of meditation, although the two terms are often used interchangeably or together, as in *mindfulness meditation*.

In the simplest terms, meditation and mindfulness do two things: (1) allow you to calm the mind; and (2) allow you to be fully present – or to focus your attention on just one thing at a time.

And in a Busy as F*ck world, where our attention is constantly scattered, those things are priceless.

But I Can't Sit Still

While the benefits of meditation are well-documented, many still struggle with the concept: *It's too boring. It's too eastern for me. I can't sit still that long. I don't need MORE time with my thoughts.*

If that's you, hold those thoughts for a while. There are many ways to get the benefits of meditation without learning from a script or following a set of rituals. You don't have to study in India. You don't have to sit cross-legged on a beach. You don't have to chant a mantra. You don't have to do anything you don't want to.

But you owe your mind an emotional education. It's not fair to send it out into the world without relaxation skills and discipline. It's far too easily led. Give it a chance to show you what it can do.

So ask yourself if you can answer '*yes*' to a single question:

Can you quiet your mind?

214

To expand, can you stop those wayward thoughts? Shut down your inner critic? Halt those worries that spin into a self-destructive loop, which always land in the same place – slamming your self-worth. Can you wind down mentally without using physical activity? Can you sit still in peace?

Or is your mind calling the shots? Is it running *you*?

If you are a chronic worrier or over-thinker, then you need to get your mind working for – not against – you. It's time to put it on a leash (not a choke chain, because you still want to be creative and spontaneous) so that it can't do whatever it wants, wreaking havoc along the way.

Interested? Check out these proven benefits:

- Psychological relief. Reduces anxiety and depressive symptoms, calms you down, helps free you from negative thoughts. Can help you hit pause before reacting too quickly or inappropriately.
- Physiological benefits. Lower blood pressure, slower heart rate, reduction in other physical symptoms of stress. Also, improved sleep and energy levels.
- Improved concentration. Obvious benefits for home, work, study, competition and other activities that require you to focus. Huge in the area of peak performance.
- Present-moment living. Living right here, right now should be everyone's mantra. Leads to improved relationships, better work habits, more fun.
- Security in your back pocket. Knowing you can call on mindfulness techniques whenever things start to spin out of control is a built-in security system.
- Reduced distraction. Or at least a pathway back to the present.
- Fuller life experience. More bang for your life's buck.

Who wouldn't you want a piece of that? But how to go about it? Here's a simple exercise to get you started:

Mindfulness for the (Slightly) Suspicious

Mindfulness is the cool kid on the meditation block, mostly because it can be adapted for use in so many settings: home, work, sport, competition, exams and schools – anywhere you need to calm down, sharpen your focus and be right here, right now. It is keenly sought by corporates, elite athletes wouldn't (or shouldn't) be without it and it is now being introduced to primary schools where kids' anxiety is ramping up.

But unlike other commodities, you can't shell out a few dollars, set up mindfulness in the lounge, sit back on the sofa and press play. You have to learn and practise it. It's like taking your emotional self to the gym. You can't go once and expect to be fit.

So how can you learn it quickly? It's a fair question because we all want the shortcut keys to anything if we can get them.

So here's a short route to mindfulness, with due respect to the masters of the craft, who have spent years refining it. This is a simple mindfulness mediation exercise. (Note that there are lots of phone apps for this – some are great except for one thing: they keep you on your phone. So here's something you can do all by yourself.)

1. Bring the attitude.
Stop saying mindfulness is boring, how it's better suited to monks in the Himalayas than to you, that you don't want to sit still for long. Going in with an open mind is the first step in getting any benefits (from anything).

2. Sit down.
Many mindfulness techniques are built around walking or other daily activities but it's easiest to start by sitting still in a comfortable position. (You don't have to close eyes, cross legs or assume a pose).

3. Focus.

Begin with an object placed in front of you – something solid you can see and describe. Roses and candles are the cliché but anything is fine. (Keep the same object for subsequent meditations of this type, at least initially.) You can hold the object if this feels more natural.

4. Breathe.

As you look at the object, steady your breathing. There are no set rules and a raft of different techniques, but a simple box breathing technique is a good starting point. It's called box breathing to represent the four sides of a box and works like this: breathe in for a count of four (hold for a count of four), then breathe out for a count of four (and hold for a count of four). Repeat several times.

5. Observe.

Bring the object into focus. Sharpen the focus. Brighten the colour. Make it vivid. Notice all the details in the object: colour, texture, size, shape, etc. Keep your breathing steady.

6. Describe.

Methodically describe all the details you can see, smell and feel. Not out loud. This keeps your attention here and now *and* makes it hard for negative (or any) thoughts to scamper back in.

7. Release.

As you breathe, feel the tension leave your body.

8. Repeat (optional).

Once is enough for beginners – and keep it short. Five minutes at the start – whatever you can manage. And once a day is fine; it is better to aim to form a steady habit before extending it.

A Note for Chocolate Lovers

Some people use a piece of chocolate or other sweets as their object because it adds taste and touch to the experience. This is fun but not to be used every time, for obvious reasons!

***

Remember, mindfulness has centuries of evidence in its corner. If you want the benefits, they're yours and they're free. But don't expect mindfulness to come after you. It already likes the life it's got.

Ready to Design Your Life?

DJ, a professional fisherman, wants to get straight down to business.

'None of that touchy-feely stuff for me,' he says when we meet. 'Although I could probably do with some. I know what I want to do with my life, I just need a solid plan for getting there.'

DJ is, by his own description, a 'river rat' who has followed the trajectory for happiness in the most traditional way: discover your passion early and find a way to make money from it. He was barely walking when he caught his first trout and from that moment on fishing was a huge part of his life – if not everything.

Every day after school he would grab his tackle and head to the water – the river was his favourite, but any form of fishing would do. When his mates lost interest he hauled on the waders in all weathers, building knowledge of the best fishing spots, lines and flies, even developing his own.

Fishing had been, DJ says, an escape from his grim home life. His mother had died before he started school; his father was a man of few words, worked almost non-stop and never asked where DJ had been even when he got home soaked and after dark. 'Most parents would have been horrified at the risks I took – I nearly drowned twice – but I could do what I wanted, no questions asked. The river was my place. It was where I felt free.'

Two decades on, the interest DJ had poured himself into as a boy is yielding healthy profits: he runs guided river-fishing tours for tourists, has an online store, a money-making blog, a series of teaching videos and plans for expansion into other countries.

He has banged up against a lot of critics: mates who hadn't been so driven and were leading the kinds of lives he doesn't want; other fishermen envious of his business acumen (and money).

'Tell me about the rest of your life?' I ask, seeking context. In order to coach someone with their goals you need some perspective around where they sit in relation to everything else. 'Do you have a partner? Kids?' In his early 30s, he's a good-looking man, confident and likeable with a quick sense of humour. 'I can't seem to make that side of things work,' he says, admitting there'd been a lot of women. Fleetingly.

He says his relationships never lasted beyond a few months; he backed off when they started wanting 'too much from me'. He'd gained weight recently because he ate on the run, no longer had time for the boxing gym and spent every waking minute on his work. 'I'm a boring bastard,' he says.

'Is that who you want to be?'

He grins. 'Happiness can't buy money – but I take your point.'

DJ had left school early and had no formal qualifications. He had picked up everything he needed along the way – technical, marketing and financial skills. But everything else had been neglected.

When I ask what's important to him as a man, he doesn't respond. 'I mean, when you get to the end of your life is your business the only thing you want to have done? Because if it is, that's fine. We can set fishing goals.'

'Fishing's not all I'm about,' he says, crossing his arms. I can't help noticing an image looking suspiciously like a rainbow trout inked into one bulky forearm.

'No shame in it if you are,' I counter. 'I just need to know.'

He sits quietly for a long time. 'This is exactly what I need.'

The Art of Looking Up

All we have to do is decide what to do with the time that is given to us – JRR Tolkien

One of the great rewards of working with people is helping to design and build the lives they truly want. Who do you want to be? Who do you want in your world? How do you want your future to look? How are we going to get there?

DJ didn't have any particular personality vulnerability, but his singular focus was causing him to neglect other areas of his life. He measured himself by the size of his bank account because, he said, he was terrified of being broke – his family had so little money growing up. But while he had sought help with business planning, he quickly realised he needed to set that plan within a bigger picture for himself.

DJ's here-and-now approach is hugely common in a Busy as F*ck world, especially when we are satisfied (or vaguely so) with where we're at. It's easier to focus on the present: on working hard, meeting our personal demands, smashing through the to-do list and ripping into whatever's happening at the weekend. And, to be fair, that smiling photo of you frolicking at the beach is going to get more 'likes' on Instagram than the one of you in sweatpants, wearing a Socratic expression, trying to plan your future.

While I agree with living in the moment, it's not helpful if it stops you from looking up and out. And it's not smart if it means you neglect, or avoid, thinking about your future and planning for your life.

Therapy focuses rightly on the present and dips into the past, but arguably doesn't spend enough time on the future, on building a hopeful view of what lies ahead, before locking down a plan to get there. I like to think everyone I work with, before they stride through the exit door, gets a chance to think beyond their day-to-day struggles, to dream about, and plan for, the person they want to be and the life they want to have. Because if you are able to lock in a vision of the future you are very often able to achieve it, alongside (or in spite of) all the other challenges life throws at you.

People get excited at the idea of designing their futures. But it can be a challenging task, a bit like being asked what you want for your birthday. You don't like to ask for too little because you want the best possible gift. But you don't like to ask for too much because it could end in disappointment. And you'll also sound greedy.

So you pitch in the middle; you try to be reasonable.

But this is your life.

Why do you have to be reasonable?

***

I encourage people to push the boat out.

Come on, dream big. What would you really like from your life?

When I first started in this work I thought I'd have to rein people in, to bring some realism to the table. Hmmmm. Do you think an Olympic track gold medal is possible when you don't like to run? If you want to win world mastermind shouldn't you start with a pub quiz? A year of travelling the world sounds fantastic but you might need to set up a travel fund.

But I've never had to do that.

Most people dream small. Despite all the self-help advice out there pushing the setting of wildly audacious goals, and telling us we can be anything we want to be, most people play it safe. They keep things realistic, achievable. Perhaps because they don't want to fail. Or because going bold may turn the volume up on that nasty little voice in their head: no you can't, no you can't, no *you* can't. Leave that to someone cooler, smarter, more qualified, better looking – and definitely thinner.

A few people have fun with the task. My dream is to win the Mega Millions lottery. Then they'll laugh, not because it's funny, just because they want you to know they are not stupid. I actually did work with a woman who had won a jackpot of several million dollars – our work was on how to cope with life two years after the win, which she said had turned her into a 'bitch of the highest order'. I loved that she said that. It's not great to be a bitch. But it's all-powerful to know you are behaving like one.

Others put in orders for tropical islands or castles or mansions in the south of France but they are always joking. Young, talented athletes always want to 'turn pro' but, despite the hype, I've never heard anyone wish in advance for a reality TV career. An awful lot of young people float the idea of being a digital nomad – 'just me and my laptop traveling the world' – but I've seen a few of these young people when they've gotten home, and let's just say living the dream wasn't really a dream after all. Being lonely, broke and semi-homeless with a dodgy internet connection can prompt a rapid change of heart. A lot of people dream of having their own businesses, but that's often prompted by frustration with a job or boss, or just a cry for freedom when they feel so controlled by everything going on in their Busy as F*ck lives.

I've seen people aim for million-dollar incomes (almost always men). A few want specific cars or big toys (again, mostly men); lots of people want a partner and/or children, but some singles (especially women) are too scared to make this a written goal because they've been burned in relationships or they fear feeling like a failure if it doesn't work out.

Most people want great careers/meaningful work; some want outlets for their creativity. Lots of people (mainly women) have specific houses or decorating features in mind. They can tell you exactly how their dream house/garden would look. Young people are much more socially and environmentally conscious than previous generations; they want to make a real contribution to the world. (People who say millennials are selfish need to spend more time talking to them.) Everyone wants to travel but what they mostly mean is that they want the freedom (in time and money) to be able to travel. Good health is an interesting one, because it tends to be taken for granted. Everyone wants to be healthy in theory but unless they have had bad health they have to be prompted to put it on the list.

Some people *can't* forecast their future because they don't know how. One intelligent man who had struggled with chaotic moods, emotions and the accompanying behaviours all his life had never imagined he would get to the age of 30. He'd booked in for therapy on the eve of his 30th birthday because he'd made it. He was alive. He'd never set a goal in his life so he had no idea how to live on the other side.

Some people (almost always young) *won't* forecast their future because they don't like what they see. Divisive leaders, political jousting, countries at war, social injustices, environmental sabotage, terrorism. 'What's the point?' they'll say. The world's going to hell anyway.

Some people *struggle* to forecast their future because they only know what they don't want. One woman, an empty-nester who'd just turned 50 and wanted her mojo back, wrote down what she wanted for the next 30 years, based on everything she didn't want. It was, if I may say so, a mood-killing list.

'So if that's the life that you create for yourself, will you be happy?'

She sat there, contemplating it for what felt like a long time. 'That list makes me feel like vomiting.' Then she burst out laughing. 'I have homework to do,' she said.

Free the Artist Within: How to Spark Your Imagination (and Why You Should)

'What do you do creatively?' I asked this woman.

She stared back a little sourly, like I'd breached some sort of therapeutic etiquette. 'What do you mean?' she said. 'I can't draw. I'm not imaginative. I don't think like that. I'm not arty, I'm a *practical* person.'

It's a common response to this question but it's one that needs to be asked – particularly when people feel stuck – because tapping into your creativity is the best way I know of shuffling out of the gloom. It doesn't have to be huge either. You just have to 'make stuff'.

I once listened to a colleague explaining depression to her nearly 80-year-old dad. He didn't understand. 'I don't know why people get so down,' he said. 'They should just go out into the shed and make something.'

After a few years of therapeutic work I understood the truth of his words.

Psychologists have to be careful here. It would be irresponsible to cite 'making stuff' as a substitute for the specialist intervention required to treat moderate to severe depression. But you can't work with people therapeutically over many years and fail to notice creative expression is vital to robust health – both physical and mental. And to stifle it is to risk sickness and malaise.

Researcher and storyteller, Dr Brené Brown, goes further: 'Unused creativity is not benign. It festers, it metastasizes into resentment, grief and heartbreak.'

Sickness, really? It initially struck me as a big call to align (not using) creativity with harmful illness, such as a cancer.

Yet it reminded me of the many unwell people I've seen over the years who had let their creativity dry up or – perhaps even worse –

had never tapped into it. And the even greater number who, once they engaged in ideas, in using their hands and practical skills, began to feel better, healthier and more alive.

But I Can't Draw!

Many who claim a lack of creativity can track their Art Scars to childhood.

Brown's research showed 85% of people (surveyed) remembered an event at school so shaming it changed how they thought of themselves and the rest of their lives. And half of them said their shame wounds related to creativity – being dismissed, embarrassed or belittled in their attempts to 'make things'.

For those who carry creative wounds into adulthood, it can be a source of regret or deep resentment. Sadly, it can also lead you to close down your imagination, to think and behave by rote, so your days are drained of colour and life.

Equally, using your imagination to make things can distract you from your problems, keep you in the present moment, allay your overthinking and fill your time constructively.

Making stuff is the simplest mindfulness exercise of all.

To have a new experience, to bring something into the world that has been dreamt up or made by you, can bring a sense of accomplishment you can't get any other way. It's a means, however small, of making your own unique mark on the world.

Too many of us deny our creativity with statements like those of the woman I was working with. But we need to put away the excuses. People who say they're a 'practical person' are either not tapping into their own source or not noticing it when they do. It's never too late to open up your imagination or, if it's been dormant, give it a reboot.

Here's a simple exercise to help:

- Write down all the activities you enjoy doing (e.g. coding, cooking, sports, outdoor pursuits and games, playing with kids, Lego/model making, sewing, crafts, doodling, designing/organising your house, building, gardening, fitness training, cleaning, running your business, driving or working on your car, writing poems, blogging, playing music and so on).
- Pick one of them and brainstorm one fresh way you could approach it. Say, try a new recipe or pattern; a better, faster, more efficient, more attractive way of doing or making something? Add a new exercise to your training or a new component to your business?

If it feels hard or stressful, trace or copy someone else's work or use a pre-made pattern and just join the dots. Whatever it is, you'll put your own spin on it. And if you don't get a buzz out of it, try something else – and challenge yourself to keep going.

Tapping into your creativity is not a catch-all cure for depression, even though therapists repeatedly see the evidence it offers for improved mental health. But if you neglect the artist within, whatever he or she looks like, you're denying yourself one of the most powerful natural medicines of all.

Two Dirty P Words: Passion and Purpose

When we talk about designing a life, two words come up over and over again: passion and purpose. People want them or need them or don't have them or are still looking for them. I listen, I nod, but then I change the language and find another way because they're not helpful. Here's why.

Passion

There's a famous kids' story called *We're Going on a Bear Hunt*. A father and his kids go out in a state of high excitement seeking the bear. They trek over all sorts of terrain, in all sorts of weather (wearing only T-shirts) but when they discover the bear in a cave they freak out and run home: the hunt was not what it seemed. And there might be a bit more involved in taming a bear than they thought.

So it is with passion. Everyone wants to hunt that bear down because it looks like the key to inspired living, but the hunt almost never turns out as planned. Even if you find your passion, you can't just grab it from its cave and take it home for a happy life. You have to work with it, and on it, for a very long time, often at the cost of other aspects of life.

Still, the hunt for passion remains the dream for so many – the magic elixir that, once you sip from the cup, all will be well.

I wish I had a passion.

I haven't yet found my passion.

I need to find something I'm passionate about.

If only I had something I could throw myself into.

He's lucky to have such a passion.

While it's fantastic to know your life's higher calling, to throw your heart into your activities and to do what you love every day, that's not how it works for most people. Most of us are not born on an arrow-like mission to be the person we are born to be. We're not springing from bed the moment the alarm goes off so we can set the world alight in our own unique ways. Most of us are getting up to the ordinary chaos of life, to all the problems we've struggled to block out overnight.

We need time, misfires, wrong turns and perspective to figure out what lights us up. And thinking about the passion we don't have causes more distress than joy.

The opportunity to be passionate lies in front of us daily; it is about the attitude and energy we bring to our lives. The trouble is, we frequently hold back because whatever we are doing, whoever we are with, is Not Really Us. It's just a holding pen until we discover our true destiny. That career. That relationship. That weight loss. That house. That inheritance. That fascinating new hobby. That thing that will make everything right.

Holding out leads us to live with one foot in and one foot out. I don't really want to be with this person. I don't really want to work in this job. I don't really want the life I have landed in. *But* I don't have a better option right now. I'll just wait and see what happens ...

And the clock ticks on.

Purpose

I don't ask people about their life's purpose because it's too much like passion: when they don't know what theirs is it makes them more stressed – and when we're trying to reduce those feelings, that's not helpful. Some people know exactly why they're on earth but they are the minority. Most of us are just here, doing our best and trying to make the best of whatever time we have. We're not Florence Nightingale or Mahatma Gandhi or Pablo Picasso or Marie Curie so we don't need the pressure of having to state our One True Mission.

But sometimes it's helpful to throw a few big questions on the table just to get people thinking in the right direction for life planning. These are my favourites; see if you can answer them:

- What do you do without looking at the clock?
- What activity do you sneak back to when no-one is watching?
- What makes you feel alive? What makes your heart thump?

- What hurts you (and how much are you exposed to it)?
- In what ways do you limit yourself?
- What do you long for?
- How could you add more regular fun to your life (being realistic)?
- In which areas of your life do you need to wake up and be honest?
- What have you been neglecting?
- What's good about your life right now?
- Who do you most enjoy being with? Do you spend enough time with them?
- What are you good at? What have you been complimented on?
- What would you need to do (or stop doing) to make yourself proud?
- What are you looking forward to? This week? This month? This year? In five years?
- Who and what will be important to you 10 years from now?

***

Some people find those easy, but most don't. It doesn't matter: it's just a starting point. Once you've had a think about what matters to you, it's time to draw your map.

The Parachute of Dreams (a Foolproof Map for Your Life)

The great thing about this parachute is that there's no risk – it always opens. Well, unless you don't want it to. You *do* have to open it yourself.

***

I come from a family of goal setters.

Every January all of us – parents, brothers, sisters, partners, kids – submit a list of targets, serious and fun, we plan to go after in the next 12 months. We all get involved; there are senior and junior (still at school) categories. At the end of the year we add up the points and get together for a party. We have winners and losers; there are no participation certificates. We fail spectacularly some years, or we do great (or odd) things that weren't on the list, or life dives off course in good ways and bad – but whatever happens, we still come together to celebrate; we still eat cake.

***

Goal setting has split the self-help world. On one side sit the Demigods of Focus, the people who do not let a single thing distract them ever on the way to *success*. These people may have a lot of money in the bank but they are frequently not much fun to be around: just ask their long-suffering partners and children. On the other side are the go-with-the-flow brigade, who live by the mantra: 'throw the goals out and focus on the journey'. Feel the experience. Life is a river: go with the current. Or whatever.

In the middle is where you'll find me. Fence sitting is not my usual style but when it comes to designing your life I think it's smart. You want to know where you are going, but you need flexibility around the route you are going to take to get there. Being too rigid in pursuit of goals can prevent you from seeing doors that open right in front of you, or can keep you gnawing away at a bone that has long since been stripped clean. Also, we need flexibility to deal with any curve balls life throws at us, which can steer us down a new pathway or at least force us to hit the pause button for a while.

Some people are anti–goal setting, which needs to be respected.

I once I asked a friend on New Year's Day if she had plans for the coming year and the conversation went roughly like this:

Me: Got any resolutions or goals for the year?

Her: You know I hate that sh*t.

Me: Hmm. Okay. (I didn't know.)

Her: Resolutions are things you fail at. Goals are lists of things you never do. I don't need any more reasons to feel crap about myself.

She has a lot of supporters. While it's impossible to put exact figures on it, it's fair to say that the huge majority fail or lapse in their goals, or can't sustain changes over time. It is estimated fewer than five per cent of all goal setters write them down. Many studies have shown writing goals down at least doubles your prospect of achievement, mostly because it clarifies intention and makes it easier to prioritise your activities. But, still, most people don't want to go there: it seems contrived, boring even.

But let me plead the case otherwise. The most common reason we fall short is we set our goals randomly with a short-term focus: to 'fix' whatever's worrying us right now. We don't connect them to a higher purpose or to things that are personally meaningful to us. They could be anyone's goals. *I want to lose weight. I want to pay down debt. I want to get fit. I want to have my own business.*

The other barrier is not having a simple way of getting 'back on the horse' when things get hard or go wrong. When we don't have a process or formula for resetting, it's easy to get overwhelmed or discouraged. Or even lose track of why we set out to do this in the first place.

When we fail we (unfairly) blame our lack of willpower or discipline. But it's not that – it's that our goals, hopes and dreams are not fuelled by what matters to *us* and/or matched tightly enough to our interests.

THE PARACHUTE OF DREAMS

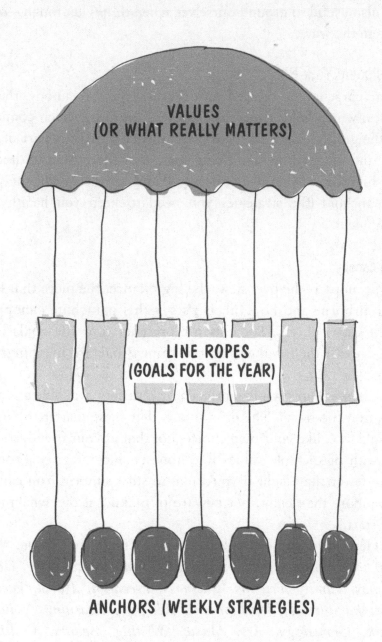

VALUES
(OR WHAT REALLY MATTERS)

LINE ROPES
(GOALS FOR THE YEAR)

ANCHORS (WEEKLY STRATEGIES)

So here is a method I've developed to make goals unique, meaningful and easy to update as we grow and change direction. It's also useful to ground ourselves when things get tough – or life gets in the way.

Designing Your Parachute

Your parachute is divided into three parts: the canopy, the line ropes, which hold it together, and the anchors, which connect it to the ground. Each of these components represents part of your life: the canopy (the high flying part, your life goals and dreams), the line ropes (where you're at now and for the rest of the year), the anchors (the strategies you need to keep you healthy and grounded).

The canopy

The canopy is the overview, the big picture, the piece that keeps you airborne and hopeful. Let's say this parachute canopy has eight strips of silk. Each strip represents your life goals (some like to call them values) or the things that are meaningful to you.

Choose your own from the endless variety available and write them on the strips. The only rule is that these matter to you – it should look like your own choice, not that of your friend, so don't go with predictable values like honesty and integrity. (You can have fewer than eight if you'd like to start simpler. You can also have more than eight, but beware of making it overwhelming at the start.)

Here are some examples: *Money. Creativity. Home. Work. (Particular) Interests. Community. Social justice. Love. Health. Money. Family. Friends. Business. Freedom. Travel. Personal growth. Spiritual development. Religion. Learning. Volunteer work. Genealogy. Art. Music. Writing. Beauty. Outdoors. Sports. Fun.*

The line ropes

I've taken some creative licence here in allowing eight ropes – one for each strip of silk. The ropes are connected to your life goals and represent this year, the current 12 months (you can start from the beginning of the year, or right now).

Set one goal for the year (or what is left of it) in each of the areas that matter to you. The logic is that if you achieve them, it will take you in the direction of your life goals; you'll be building a life that matters *to you.*

Examples:

- If your higher goal/value is *creativity* and you love to craft things out of wood (or compile a recipe book, exhibit your art or any creative project), identify a project you want to finish *this year.*
- If *family* is important to you, plan a trip to see them *this year* or hold yourself to some form of regular catch up.
- If *money* is a higher goal, write down the specific amount you want to save or pay back *this year.*
- If you want to own your own *business,* isolate at least one thing you need to do *this year* to move in that direction.

The anchors

These represent your life right now, what you do every week. This is what grounds you, and gives you a way of making progress **this week.**

These anchors are what you do weekly to move yourself in the direction of your goals. (Note: When people are struggling with their mental health, this can be used more as a form of self-care, to make sure they are doing all they can to look after themselves).

Anchors are particularly useful when you lose your way with your life goals. They allow you to put aside thoughts of failure and return immediately to your plan – and then to carry on. Without these, we tend to drift and not live purposefully.

Examples:

- Creative projects: note your activities for *this week*, what you will have completed by the end of the week.
- Running a half marathon: note your training program for *this week*. How much distance will you cover?
- Having your own business: note what you will do *this week* to increase your learning (books, podcasts, blogs, TED talks, assess your finances).
- Weight loss: note your goals for *this week* only.
- Self-care, e.g. take time out and go to a movie by yourself.

Note: it's important that when you look at your anchors they generally feel like fun, things you want to do, either for pure enjoyment or because they're the things that make you feel good if you do them every week. If you look at your anchors and feel tired or bored, you're not finished – you need to give it a little more thought.

Remember, achieving what you want in life does take a little grit and discipline. But it doesn't need to weigh you down; you shouldn't be staggering under the burden of it. You should just feel pleased you're on track, you've taken the time to map out your future and invest in yourself.

Staying on Track (or Not)

All the goal-setting literature advocates regular check-ins on our goals to make sure we are on track – or to see if we have fallen by the way (yet again) and need to hit the reset button. It's a good idea, even if it's hard to remember to do so when the days are turning over at breakneck speed.

If you don't get around to a regular check-in, it's worth putting the heat on yourself to do it at least once a year. My favourite month for this is December because it offers the best excuse for self-reflection. It's an opportunity to look back on the highs and lows of the past 12 months, to bank all the good stuff and square away all the bad. So we can muscle up to a new year with a clean and optimistic slate.

But how?

In coaching and therapy sessions, I've tried a lot of life-assessment tools. Many are either complex or onerous or, dare I say it, boring. Sometimes you just want your self-reflection straight – and over quickly.

So here's my version, complete with three of the best stripped-down questions to check in on your year and maybe even tap what's going on at the core of you.

The Dream Team: Cool, Bold and Reckless

Time left 12 fresh months in your care. How many
of them did you share with opportunity and dare ... ?
– from 'Victory' by Herbert Kauffman.

What leaps into your mind when you read this quote? Pride at all you've achieved over the last 12 months? Or is it just same old, same old *again*. Didn't lose that weight you never quite lose. Didn't knock much off that ever-increasing debt. Achieved that worthy-but-extraordinarily-dull work goal but – yawn.

Maybe it's time to try something different?

How to assess your year. If you dare.

This is a short quiz. So no need to write down your answers. You can do it solo or in a group but if you are with others be respectful of their answers. When people make themselves vulnerable we need to listen and support – not criticise. (You can be tough on yourself, though.)

What's the *coolest* thing you did this year? What's your best memory? The moment when you felt excited? Lucky? Alive?

Ha! you say. *Too easy.* You're right, it is. And I know how you'll answer too, because the roaring majority of us approach this the same way. You'll name an experience you had because it's on-trend to talk up experiences. Maybe something you saw or did on a trip or with your favourite people.

You won't mention money (even if money was the thing that enabled you to have that experience) because that's tacky and no-one wants to be tacky. Even if you've had a difficult year, you won't find this question hard. This is good because it reminds us that suffering is never all suffering – that cool stuff happens in between.

But challenge yourself as to *why* it was your coolest thing. Was it cool for cool's own sake? Or just your best, most-liked Instagram post? Something you hoped would make you look cool to someone else? Your answer should align with what matters to you.

What's the *boldest* thing you did this year? How did you push yourself? Challenge a personal fear or the status quo? Surprise yourself with your courage? Why did you do it? What did you learn or gain?

I asked some friends this. We delved into relationships, health, work, bodies and trying new things. I can't give more detail because I don't have so many friends that I can afford to betray them but they gave thoughtful answers, disclosed surprising things. It's healthy to voice your fears out loud – even if they are little ones and especially if they are big ones. Note: you should have done something bold in at least two areas of your life and if you haven't, *why not?* Are you living too quietly? Too carefully? Risk is vital to growth so put yourself under a little pressure.

What's the most *reckless* thing you did this year? Have you been rash, impetuous, daring? Been wild on a whim? Tried or said something you never thought you would?

I'm not talking about doing mean or dangerous things – acts that harm people (or yourself) or cost thousands of dollars in rescue missions. As long as you're not hurting anyone, breaking the law or smashing up against your own values, it's okay to go a little crazy sometimes. In fact, you're missing out if you don't.

We spend so much time grinding towards well-intentioned goals that really don't light us up. Or beating ourselves up for all the things we haven't done (or failed at) each year. But crazy, spontaneous acts are often the ones we remember, those that still make us smile when we're rocking out on the rest home porch.

Struggling with your answer? If you can't name a single out-of-the-box thing you've done this year, then I'd take a punt you are bored with life. Even stuck. Am I right?

So come on, there's a whole fresh year just around the corner. It's winking at you. Promise me you'll do something reckless with it.

***

And here's one more thing to think about based on a random survey I carried out on people I work with, friends and family. I've since repeated it several times and each time the results are remarkably similar.

If you had one day left to live what would you do?

I once had a housemate who would ask me when I came in from work, 'How was your day?'

Same question every day, delivered with a smile. At first I answered politely. *Good, thanks*. But my resentment began to bubble: *Ask me something else. Another question. A better question. STOP ASKING ME THIS STUPID QUESTION.*

You've guessed the problem here. It was not her question; it was my answer – or lack of an interesting one. I did not like my job; I did not like my boss; I did not like my circumstances. I felt stuck, riding a conveyor belt to a boring old age. And her daily probe threw the spotlight on it.

Back then, in my mid-20s, I fervently believed a wasted day would lead to a wasted life. I've since learned it doesn't at all – unless you let them pile up.

We each have our own ideas on what makes a great day. Wellbeing experts cite the following key ingredients: be present, finish something, connect with others, declutter, do less, do something you've been putting off, be kind, be grateful, look after your body and record a happy memory.

Worthy, but where's the decadence in that? Call me an outlier but my ideal day would never include finishing a tax return or cleaning out a closet – especially if I had only one day left.

So I decided to carry out an informal study. There was no research model to follow, no forms to fill in, no control group, limited diversity in the sample (and everyone had the basic safety, shelter and hunger needs met).

I just asked every adult I talked to (27 in total) two questions:

1. What is your idea of a perfect day?

Then …

2. How much would this change if you had 24 hours to live?

The simplicity of the findings surprised me. In creating a perfect day, three things sprung from the pack:

Eat great food

Most people found a place for their favourite food or a great meal. Brunch was the clear winner, topped by eggs benedict and the Big Breakfast. French fries rated more than one mention. And a glass of wine or a cold beer at the end of the day made the cut for a lot of my sample.

Feel calm

You won't find this on any official lists but almost everyone mentioned it; perhaps it reflects the stress we're feeling on a daily basis. Answers included: *Start the day slowly. Sleep in or wake up in my own time (without an alarm). No stress. No rushing. No time constraints. Feeling in control of my day. Having time to talk when I drop the kids at day care. A day where the kids don't fight. A facial, a massage – something just for me. Sitting with my partner in comfortable silence.*

Go outside

Get into nature. Feel the sun on my skin. Hiking. Walking. Cycling. Trail running. Fishing. Golf. Picnics (probably should be filed under food). Playing casual sports with my family. Perhaps not surprisingly, most people ordered sunshine.

But with One Day to Live?

Would the picture change? Not as much as you'd think, although the requests for 'me time' fell away. As one woman put it, 'I'd drop all the selfish stuff, spend the day with my family and eat fries.'

Food

Food again came in at number one. I asked some people if it was about food being a social thing – but most said no, it was just that food was delicious. Most popular: fish on the barbecue. Gourmet burgers. Something with bacon. More fries. So, apparently, our last supper does matter.

People
Most people wanted to bring together loved ones. Record happy memories to leave behind. One woman wanted four funerals – so she could have four lots of laughs with her favourite people – but she wouldn't risk bringing them all together at once in case they fought. But most people closed ranks: they only wanted those closest to them. Family didn't always beat friends; kids mostly came in ahead of partners.

Warmth
Again, this was people-related. Smiles, laughter, hugs, no conflict, a few prayers. This seemed related to how they wanted to leave things – in peace.

Other interesting responses: only one person considered going to work, and only one wanted to jet off to a foreign country but that was about seeing something new for the last time. One young woman wanted to see as many dogs as she could. More men than women wanted to end the day with sex. Just saying. One man wanted it twice.

Perhaps the most poignant answer came from a woman who said she would patch up a rift with a sibling; they used to be very close.

'This is making me emotional,' she said. 'But when I die I'd like to have everything, all my relationships, in a good place.

She paused and dabbed at her eye. 'What am I waiting for?'

– SESSION 10 –

Licensed to Live
(Because Then We Die)

Don't cry because it's over, smile because it happened.
– Dr Seuss

Livvy is ready to leave therapy.

You met Livvy at the start of this book. She skidded into my office in a high state of agitation, her eyes darting around the room; she could barely sit still for an entire hour. Just looking at her increased my heart rate.

She was as Busy as F*ck.

Now she's here for her last session. She hasn't had a panic attack for months, her anxiety has settled, she is eyeing an exciting new job and she is about to step out of the room into the rest of her life.

I'm excited for her, but I'll miss her. That's the thing about being a psychologist: just because you want people to live happily without you, doesn't mean you enjoy it.

'So it's over,' she says. 'This is where you say something wise and illuminating that will sustain me all the rest of my days.'

'Ha. No pressure then. What if what I say is not good enough?'

She grins at the reference to her perfectionist standards, something we'd worked on. But she isn't finished with me. 'If you say goodbye and good luck, I'll slap you. I've spent a lot of time and money here and I expect the best you've got.'

She hugs me then, which some psychologists frown on but I let clients create their own ending: if they want to hug, I do too. And I promise when I get home tonight I'll write her some parting words, tips for life, boiled all the way down. Those words led me to write this book and you'll find them on the last page.

***

We Say Goodbye

So that's it. You've read the book, tried some of the tools, held on to the ones that worked for you, discarded those that didn't. And even if you haven't put any of them into action yet, hopefully you have some fresh ideas about making change, coping with stress (and crap), and navigating the Busy as F*ck world we live in. Most of all, I hope you feel more optimistic about the life you have – or the one you can create.

Good psychological health is not the absence of stress, anxiety or depression. It's not about how hard you work or how many emails you get while on holiday. It's not about how many races you win, how clean your house is or how successful your kids are. It's definitely not about how much you weigh. It's about surviving life's challenges and thriving alongside them. It's about taking charge of the things you can and letting the rest go. It's about living a full (but not insanely so) and enriched life. It's about getting to know, and feeling good about, yourself, having warm relationships with people who you like (and who like you back), doing something that's meaningful to you and having a few laughs along the way.

It's about getting the Busy as F*ck years in order because, either way, they're taking your youth, energy and health with them.

***

I don't like saying goodbye. From the outset my aim is to make myself spectacularly unnecessary – but when you have worked with people so intensely it's hard to let go.

People tend to think the therapy room is a conveyor belt of distress, that one person follows another and when each leaves, we bring the red rubber stamp down on their file, print 'discharged' and move briskly to the next in line.

That's not it at all. Each person leaves their mark. Sometimes it's a scuff mark, sometimes it's a crevice, sometimes it's a lump in your throat you can't quite swallow. Always it's their story. Their pain. Their vulnerability. Their progress. Their joy. Their freedom from panic attacks. Their new lover or rekindled marriage. A grateful email from their partner or a parent. Occasionally, it's a thoughtful card or gift. Once I got a melting ice-cream. I still have a bottle of desert sand from one of my earliest clients, a Jordanian refugee who escaped a violent marriage. And on my wall hangs a red koru, signalling new beginnings, from a young woman who was determined to put her traumatic past to rest.

There's always something left behind.

Even when it hasn't gone well, you feel something: yes, there may be relief that it's over but there's also: What happened there? Why didn't that work? What could I have done better? And what will they say about me out in the world?

Every therapist has had people they haven't managed to help, who haven't liked them. That can be tough – it's human to want approval – but the simple truth is that not everyone will like you (and some people will not like you at all). It is perhaps life's biggest lesson, and one we should pay attention to when it's first handed to us in the school playground because it would save so much trouble.

One young woman told me her previous therapist, a hugely empathetic woman I happened to know and like, had been her fairy godmother. With my more direct approach, I didn't dare ask what she thought of me. She let me have it anyway. 'You're the black fairy,' she said, and I smiled, knowing I was lucky to even make fairy status. I also knew our work was done. As in life, it is almost impossible to have a close relationship with someone when their head is full of someone else.

Working in brief therapy means you mostly get the chance to plot the ending, to prepare well for it. And you don't have to slam the door – 'Okay, this is it, we'll never see each other again.' You can leave it ajar for a return. Some of my most fun sessions have been in catching up with people I haven't seen in years, even when difficult things have happened for them in between.

But when the ending comes swiftly, unexpectedly, it can leave you feeling shaken, bereft.

***

I've never had a client suicide.

This is not something that gives you bragging rights. I've never mentioned it before and no-one ever likes to ask. The main reason is that I haven't worked extensively in places where suicide rates are high, like psychosis services or hospitals or corrective settings. Unlike some of my colleagues, I've never had to wake up to the news that a client has taken their own life; I've never had to face their partners and parents, to wonder what else I could have done to prevent it. I've never had to live alongside it.

I've been awfully close, though, and I still think about those people.

I've sat with a man in a bare, white hospital room, with the rain thundering on the window as he tried to describe the anguish of his psychosis in pencil sketches: being squeezed to death by a giant hand, metal cuffs around his neck, drowning in a heavy ocean. I did my best to remind him of all the reasons he had to stay alive, of who'd miss him terribly if he was gone: his partner, his kids, his many friends, his eight-year-old German shepherd. He was able to name them all; he agreed he had so many reasons to live. Later that night he tried to hang himself from his bedhead with a stolen dressing gown cord.

The night orderly stopped him, not me.

I've had a barrage of late-night text messages from a frantic woman who worried her severely depressed husband was not on a 'hunting trip' at all. She was right but he changed his mind and came home at dawn. I've known a girl to renege on plans to kill herself only because she saw the sad eyes of her spoodle looking up at her. And a young man whose lethal stash of pills was discovered by his mother on the night he planned to die.

That they lived had nothing to do with me.

I've seen the washout of suicide many times; I've tried to comfort people I don't know and explain to them the inexplicable actions of people I don't know. I've seen a young man who developed a chronic stutter and a debilitating cannabis habit after finding his girlfriend swinging from the rafters in their bedroom.

I've seen the lost sons and daughters of sad people who died too young and too early, powerless to stop themselves and understand the trail of agony, all the questions, they were leaving behind. I've worked with police officers and firefighters called to bloodied suicide scenes, who had to pick fingers and toes out of the front grills of cars, who for weeks, months, afterwards would wake up with images of dead bodies raw in their minds. Or be too afraid to walk through parks in case they see a body hanging from a tree.

I've had clients die too. Cancer. Accidents. Chronic illness.

I've held it together for their families because that's the job. I remember one young woman I'd seen after her relationship broke up, coming up to me at a street festival in another town a couple of years later. Her skin was stretched thin over her small frame and she was frailer than I remembered. She wore a baseball cap. 'I have a terminal brain tumour,' she said. She was in her early 20s. I tried to mask my shock and chat naturally but how do you end a conversation like that? Nice to see you. Good luck with that. What do you say to her stoic mother, a woman you have only just met, who is standing at her shoulder? *I wish the fuck it could be different.*

A man who had come to see me for help with goal setting had a chronic physical health condition. It was well-managed but he had gained a significant amount of weight, which he was keen to work on as well as lock in a bigger plan for his life. I admired his upbeat attitude and willingness to work on himself when his physical health problems took so much energy. We had several sessions before he had to go out of town for work. I hadn't seen him for several months when I heard he'd drowned, heroically as it happened, successfully rescuing a young schoolgirl, but he was still gone.

A year later when I was searching the images on my phone I found a photo we'd taken of his goals and I'd forgotten to transfer to his file. It was titled simply 'Matt's goals': 1. Fit my jeans. 2. Go on a date.

I deleted the photo then I sat down and let the tears well up.

***

There are great endings too.

There are people for whom you know it's time to leave, that you'll never see again because you don't need to. There are others you'll think about on and off for years. Some email you with updates. Some rush up to you years later and tell you amazing stories of things that have happened: new partners, renovated bodies, career changes, unwell or unhappy children who have grown up, graduated, had babies of their own.

It is circle of life stuff, and I love hearing these stories.

I love hearing that people heal – even if they don't forget.

I love these reminders that life, even in suffering, doesn't have to be all suffering. That you can still have a belly laugh on a bad day. That good things still happen if you create space for them.

I ran into a woman in the street the other day whom I hadn't seen for a year or more. She was great fun and we'd worked together on and off for several years. In the end she was doing so well our sessions were more like a catch-up between friends. She discharged because she'd run out of excuses to keep coming back. 'I feel like I've lost a friend,' she said.

So did I. I badly wanted to ask her for coffee – but I didn't. It's not a friendship. It can't be because, even if it was permissible, it wouldn't work – not for the client and not for me. For therapeutic work, I find it easier to stay inside boundaries: the safety of the four walls and the 55-minute time frame. I once tried to do walk therapy with a young man who requested it. We walked and talked for an hour and I found it extraordinarily difficult to get my pace and pitch right. I think I talked too much. I think I wasn't supportive enough. I think I was too challenging but – this is the thing that bothers me most – I couldn't tell. I lost my radar. It didn't surprise me when the client abruptly ended our relationship during that period. He came back in time but – lesson learned – we stayed inside.

Whenever I've seen people, former or current clients, outside the room I haven't been able to shake the feeling that I'm disappointing them. That without the containment of the room, without me dedicated to their cause – and to offering up ways to comfort them and make their world easier – I'm not as valuable to them. Or as interesting. Or giving off the right realistic-optimistic vibe.

While no-one has ever said so, I think they feel it too. They don't want coffee; they want the feelings we created in the room and that they took from there out into the world. And maybe I want them too.

Friendship needs to start on even ground. After working with someone, I know almost everything about them – their families, their friends, their aspirations, their challenges, what they eat and like to do, how often they have sex (and who with). They know almost nothing about me and, even if they would genuinely like to get to know more, I wouldn't know how to let them.

So things are best left as they are.

Every therapeutic relationship is deep; secrets are held and revealed, dust and dirt left on the floor. It is a journey, and an intense one. I've had so many clients say they hate small talk at parties, that they long to have more of the kind of deep and meaningful talks we have in our work. But I think they haven't fully realised that their real interest in those conversations springs from the opportunity to talk freely about themselves, their hopes and dreams, who they truly are.

But me? I long for the banter of real, light-hearted life. When I shut the door on the day, I need to shut the door on the people behind it. It took me a long time to learn that skill but I'm good at it now. When I walk away, I don't want to talk about myself. I don't want to worry about the uncertain world we live in. I don't want to dive down deep into anything. I just want to drink some wine, have a laugh and peer out at the world through rose-tinted glasses, even though I know there's no such thing.

Spray Tans, Bikini Wax and Letting Go

I'll leave the last word to a woman I met just after her husband left her for a woman with a $29 spray tan and a French bikini wax.

'Bastard,' she said. 'He met her at *our* gym. She's 25 years old and about a size two. Her tits still point north without a bra. How can I compete with that?'

After the initial rage – she burned his suits and slashed his car tyres – she settled into a deep gloom. She kept going to work but she stopped seeing friends, she cleaned her house obsessively, she was in bed every night by 8 pm – even on weekends. She gained weight, then lost it, alternating diets and binges with maniacal gym sessions. And all the time she waited – hoped – for the return of a man who had emotionally abused her for years.

Therapy loped along for months, then years. She couldn't afford to come often so we'd meet every few months; occasionally, she'd book an emergency session just to 'get back on track'. I worried about her. She said she wasn't suicidal but I suspected she stockpiled pills and she was increasingly careless about her safety. She'd drive without a seatbelt; she'd walk along the riverbank at night. 'I just can't see the point in being here,' she would say.

Six years after her husband left, it happened: she met someone. She booked a session to share the good news.

'He's amazing,' she said. 'I've never felt like this – not even when I was 16.' The session passed as though it was seconds and it struck me how much love can change a person's presence, the energy they carry into the world. I can always feel their mood in the room; the shadow or light, the grey or colour they bring in. She felt almost weightless on this day and I found myself tapping one foot on the floor to keep myself present. I hoped she didn't think I was in a hurry to end the session.

'You're wonderful,' she said, hugging me tightly as she left. 'I'll never forget all you've done for me.' Then she stepped back. 'I'll never be back. You know that, don't you?' Sometimes I hear that and nod, disbelieving. But this time, something about her conviction made me sure. She didn't need me anymore.

She left in a cloud of perfume and I stood for a moment, smiling: I hadn't been any kind of wonderful. All I had done was sit there, year after year, encouraging her to let go of a man who had never been good for her, suggesting she deserved more.

Sometimes the job is just about being steady for someone, holding their pain, until they are ready, and strong enough, to let go.

In the end, the work is not yours to do. Nor yours to claim. Sometimes the best you can do for someone is hang on.

Sometimes, when we're truly tested, all any of us can do is hang on.

***

When I walk to work, from my suburb down through Wellington's leafy Bolton Street cemetery, I pass a gravestone that speaks to me louder than the others. It belongs to a woman named Dinah, who was married to a man named William and died in 1891. She was 56 years old. I don't know if she had children or not, or if she outlived them or not. I don't know if she had a job outside the home. I don't know if she worried about her weight. I don't know anything else about her. Her epitaph simply says this: 'Here lies Dinah, beloved wife of William. She hath done what she could.'

That's all. I imagine her, a steady capable woman, a life stripped of frills, just a cracked cream headstone in the grass, marking what would have been a difficult life, a fact I know for sure, because all lives are.

We make the world too complex as we stress and strive to be cooler, richer, more popular, more successful, more attractive, more socially acceptable and, don't forget, thinner. The further you go, the more futile it seems, because all we can do is live our best, and love our best, between the hour we are born and the hour time is called on us.

Every time I see that gravestone, it brings me home. I hope that when the end comes I'm free of to-do lists and labels, especially those bestowed by people who didn't like me much.

Here lies an Ordinary Person. She hath done what she could.

The Busy as F*ck Person's Guide to Life

Here's a snap guide to help keep you on track and sustain you when you fall off it. And if you're standing in a bookstore scanning the last page because you're too Busy as F*ck to read a whole book, steal these points and run.

Crap Happens

Crap happening to you is as certain as death – and it comes first. No matter how cool or blessed you think you are, you'll be tested. So arm yourself; stay open to change and keep building yourself an emotional toolkit that will see you through the tough times.

Date Yourself (Because It's the Only Relationship You Can't Leave)

Okay, not exclusively; that would be weird. Nurture your mind, body and spirit – and take yourself out for some fun sometimes. Yours is the only relationship you can't leave. Treat it with kindness and respect.

Keep Your Past Behind You

We all have histories, some nastier than others. Invest in understanding yours but don't let it trap you and hold you back. Life is right here, right now, so commit to being in the present while planning for the future.

Show Up and Show Off

Life is like a lottery ticket: you can't win if you're not in. So get out of bed, turn up and offer up the best you have. If you don't know what your best is, spend time working out your strengths: they're your passport to making a unique stamp on the world.

Make Bad Art

Seriously. Creativity is soul food. Don't tell yourself you're not imaginative, just make stuff. It'll distract you from you problems, ground you in the present and give you a sense of accomplishment. And if you're paralysed by your own lofty expectations, rip them down and start making *bad* art. It's really satisfying.

People Matter (But a Lot Don't)

Good relationships are the foundation of happiness. Bad ones will tear you apart and wreck your self-worth. So invest in those that matter; build a handful that will last – that will grow and change with you – and let the toxic ones go. They only serve to limit or hurt you.

Be Quite Nice

Don't be drop-dead, sickeningly nice because mean people will walk all over you. Be kind and generous but say no sometimes. Stop grovelling for attention or approval and don't dwell on what others think of you. If it helps, when you get to 50 you'll realise that no-one was all that interested in you anyway.

Your Body Is Not a Temple
Your body is just a body. So don't get all obsessed with it. Feed it well, move it and treat it with respect and it'll pay you back with strength and energy (and by fitting into your favourite clothes). Abuse it at your peril – it may just seek revenge.

Jump with Two Feet
Not off a cliff or anything dangerous, obviously. But whatever you do, do it with your whole heart. Throw yourself right over the bar. Being all-in will light you up. Being half-in, half-out in work, relationships, interests or family life will prevent you from getting the most pleasure/success/love out of anything.

Life is a Long Sprint
Statistically, all going well, and with a little luck thrown in, you will live a long time. The great temptation of youth is to *do it all now. Set goals! Be productive! Have a six-point morning routine! Read 10 books a week!* It's all good stuff but you're also allowed to lie face down, eat too much pizza and binge-watch Netflix sometimes. Take your time. Create a life that means something or leaves something. Think. Adapt. Evolve. Shuffle forward. And look for the gold in your world – even when all you can see are iron chips.

ACKNOWLEDGEMENTS

Psychology can be a challenging occupation, and writing about it a lonely one, so I'd like to raise a glass to everyone on my team. My sincere thanks to ...

- Publisher Alex Hedley and the fantastic team at HarperCollins*Publishers* New Zealand; Senior Editor Lachlan McLaine and his colleagues at HarperCollins*Publishers* Australia.
- My colleagues and friends in the world of mind health, especially Gillian Hawke for advice, support and a lot of laughs along the way.
- My friends and family, particularly my sister Lisa for the wine-infused writing retreats, my daughters for their ruthless wisdom: Kate 'B- is good enough' and Tess 'just set the book free', and my husband Kev, always. Just because.
- Finally, but not least, to all the wonderful people I have worked with over the years. The best of what I know I learned from you.

Also by Karen Nimmo

My Bum Looks Brilliant in This
(the one true secret of lasting weight loss)

Fish Pie Is Worse than Cancer